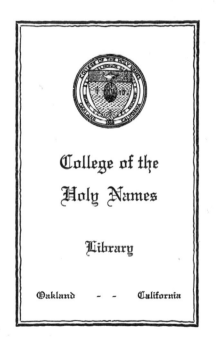

The Church-Related College

The Church-Related College

MYRON F. WICKE

Associate General Secretary
Methodist Board of Education

The Center for Applied Research in Education, Inc.
Washington, D.C.

53829

Foreword

It is impossible to understand the history of American higher education without knowing the history of the church-related colleges. For a long period of time these institutions dominated the American educational scene. The state universities and, later, the state colleges challenged their supremacy, but the enrollment in public institutions has only recently surpassed that in the church-related and independent colleges and universities.

During their long history, church colleges have not served religious purposes only; they have also contributed significantly to the making of a democratic society. Although they grew out of an aristocratic tradition, they came to provide means of social and economic mobility to the children of families of limited education and limited means. In the last two decades, however, many of the colleges have had to find a new clientele. As they raised their academic standards and, correlatively, their budgets, they had to search for students from families which could afford to pay increasingly higher fees. As a consequence, the character of the colleges has altered as they have changed their emphasis from dominantly religious to dominantly nonreligious purposes.

As they were in their beginnings, church-related colleges are still highly diverse in the characteristics of their students and of their social and educational climates. They also differ greatly in their relationships to religious denominations, and especially in the degree of control which religious bodies exercise over them. In some instances the relationship is tenuous and the control only indirect. In other cases the relationship is close and the control direct and authoritative. Dr. Wicke has properly emphasized the diversity of the institutions in control, objectives, educational programs, students, and faculties. *The* church-related college does not exist.

The church colleges have not always searched freely for the truth from whatever source it might come. Many of them were narrowly sectarian in the beginning and some still are. Many were suspicious of the intellect and some of them are afraid of it today. The best of them, however, have escaped the pettiness both of religion and of mind. These institutions do not prescribe a religious test for truth. Freely searching for the truth in all fields, they have submitted religious doctrine to scholarly examination and evaluation. In the process, they have attained academic excellence and have demonstrated the compatibility of the religious spirit and the unfettered intellect. In emphasizing learning they have not eschewed values. Instead, they have led students to face ultimate questions and to search for life's meanings.

No student of higher education is better qualified than Dr. Wicke to discuss the church-related college. As director of surveys and studies of the Division of Higher Education of the Board of Education of the Methodist Church, and in consulting capacities, he has studied more than fifty colleges of several denominations. He has thus had the opportunity to secure an intimate knowledge of a large and highly diversified group of institutions.

In addition, Dr. Wicke has been Professor of English and academic dean at two Methodist liberal arts colleges. He has taught graduate courses in higher education at the University of California and the George Peabody College for Teachers. He has also served as a trustee of five Methodist colleges. From 1958 to 1961 he was a member of the executive committee of the American Council on Education.

This rich experience qualifies Dr. Wicke to speak authoritatively on the church-related college—its government and organization, its purposes and educational program, its students and faculty, and its financial support. He is capable of outlining the conditions of its survival and, beyond that, of its excellence.

T. R. MCCONNELL
*Chairman, Center for the Study
of Higher Education*
University of California, Berkeley

The Church-Related College

Myron F. Wicke

Dr. Wicke's volume on *The Church-Related College* is in many respects a companion volume in the Library of Education to Dr. Lewis B. Mayhew's volume on *The Smaller Liberal Arts College*. Most of the colleges about which Dr. Wicke writes are liberal arts colleges, and he distinctly stresses the liberal arts point of view in his descriptions and evaluations. Central in Dr. Wicke's presentation in the idea that the institutions he is discussing are closely related to religious organizations. Extensive data specifically gathered for this study of the church-related college are presented in Dr. Wicke's book. The author provides many interesting "exhibits" or descriptions of individual institutions, to show the wide range to be found among colleges in even so sharply defined a category as those that are church-related. He finds much that needs strengthening in the colleges, particularly with respect to definition of objectives and financial support. His outlook for these colleges is, on the whole, rather optimistic.

> The future of the church-related college depends upon its ability to keep a clear view of its mission; upon its ability to find the church support needed to supplement other sources of income; and upon its success in interpreting its goals to students, faculty, constituency, and the general public.

Contents

CHAPTER I

The Problem and Its History

The purpose of this monograph is to examine critically yet sympathetically the present position and future role of the church-related college in the United States. The attempt will be made to see these institutions as part of the diverse, if not chaotic, system of American higher education today. As there is the widest diversity among colleges and universities in the United States, so is there the widest kind of variety among church-related colleges. Stanford and Western Reserve are both universities, but how different! DePauw University is a Methodist-related college in Indiana but is greatly different from Austin College in Texas, related to the Presbyterian church. No qualitative evaluation is intended in these statements. The institutions are just not alike. For this reason, representative college profiles have been used throughout this study.

"Church-related" and "denominational" are not in any sense fully descriptive terms; yet they are often misused to indicate a stereotype. Thus the word "denominational" carries with it certain popular overtones, often uncomplimentary, just as the word "secular" is sometimes misused by churchmen. In this study every effort will be made to deal with facts, not slogans. Yet interpretation cannot be avoided, nor is there any desire to do so.

The study deals primarily with two-, three-, and four-year colleges, not with universities, though there are genuine universities affiliated in one way or another with the churches. The data employed in the study itself are taken from acknowledged published sources. In addition, however, a good deal of fresh material comes directly from more than 200 questionnaires (see Appendix) filled out by college administrators. These questionnaires represent every type of institution described in the following pages. Other types of printed materials from more than 100 institutions in the group studied were also examined.

The demise of the small liberal arts college (most often a church-related institution) has been predicted for half a century by notable

1

educators such as William Rainey Harper. That so many of these colleges are still alive certainly does not guarantee their continued existence nor their right to exist. Colleges which were able to survive depressions may find it much more difficult to live through advancing inflation, especially in a day of increasingly bitter competition for faculty members. The word "bitter" is not exaggerated. Faculty strength is the certain key to the future of colleges, and finances are near the core of the problems.

Another basic problem is that of aim and purpose. The insistent question is whether or not the church-related college has in fact a unique and essential role to play in American higher education. If it does and if it can publicly and intelligently rationalize its function, support will be forthcoming. This support will never be fully adequate, as it unhappily never is in any sector of American education. If a church-related college cannot rationalize its role, the institution will not merit continued existence.

The approach of this study is to look quickly at the past; to appraise factually, as far as possible, the very complex present; and to suggest some lines of future development. The study will not neglect the serious question of whether or not the church should be engaged in higher education.

A Note on History

It is not necessary here to recount fully the church's long and tortuous development of the American college and of the college's frequent metamorphosis into the modern university. Even so, it is useful to restate briefly the general historical situation out of which modern American higher education grew.

Thomas J. Wertenbaker in his book *Princeton, 1746–1896* notes that "Education in colonial America was the child of religion." It could hardly have been otherwise. The colonials were predominantly Britishers well-acquainted with English universities, which were basically church foundations. It may be difficult for the contemporary mind to believe, but as late as 1854 there were religious tests for degrees in arts, law, and medicine at Oxford; and certain religious restrictions remained at Oxford and Cambridge until 1882.

The colonial colleges. The colonials established nine colleges before 1780, all but one of them projected by churches. Even those not actually founded by church groups were to an important degree dominated by religious bodies. The modern names of these first institutions still stand for the best in American higher education—Harvard, William and Mary, Yale, Princeton, Dartmouth, Brown, Rutgers, and Columbia. (The modern University of Pennsylvania though private has had no legal connection with a church body.) In a substantial sense these were church-state institutions, for each of them received support from public sources.

From 1780 to 1799 only about sixteen new institutions of higher education were established, but from 1800 to the beginning of the Civil War a total of 147 additional "permanent" colleges were founded, and many more were created but later closed. "Permanent," the term used by Donald G. Tewksbury in *The Founding of American Colleges and Universities Before the Civil War*, refers to a college still in existence in 1932 when the Tewksbury book was published. The early colleges mentioned previously were mainly Protestant in origin, but the Roman Catholic church was not idle in higher education. Georgetown College was founded in 1789 and The Catholic University in 1889, only 13 years after the founding of Johns Hopkins. By 1860 there were 14 permanent Catholic colleges in the United States and by 1930 there were 126. Conducted by members of the clergy, they were founded largely for the same reasons as those which led to the establishment of Protestant institutions.[1]

Why did the churches found colleges and universities? One vital answer to the question is that there were no other agencies with sufficient strength in the early days of the nation to enter the field of education. Moreover, these English-Americans based their institutions upon a pattern they knew very well—the British college, and, initially, Emmanuel College of Cambridge University. It was a part of the basic tradition that religion and education were nat-

---

[1] No account is taken in this study of the several Jewish-sponsored institutions of higher education. The reason for this exclusion is implied in the following statement from the bulletin of Brandeis University, one of the most notable of these institutions: "Brandeis University came into being because of the desire of American Jewry to make a corporate contribution to higher education in the tradition of the great American secular universities that have stemmed from denominational generosity. By choosing its faculty on the basis of capacity and creativity, and its students according to the criteria of academic merit and promise, the university hopes to create an environment which may cause the pursuit of learning to issue in wisdom."

ural partners. Thus John Wesley, Oxford scholar and theologian, spoke of keeping united the two so long disjoined: "Knowledge and vital piety."

Surely another reason for founding educational institutions is apparent in the nature of the church itself. At its best the church is a servant to society, and its schools, hospitals, homes, and social agencies are testimony that the servant motive has been real and effective.

There has been long and surely fruitless debate as to whether the first institutions were meant to be basically theological schools or whether they had broader purposes. The following suggestion from a recent history of higher education in the United States makes an important point:

> It is useless to argue whether the colonial colleges were intended to be theological seminaries or schools of higher culture for laymen. They were clearly designed for both functions, although in a strictly technical sense special vocational training for the ministry, in distinctly professional institutions, did not develop here until the nineteenth century.[2]

This point has been stated another way by Frederick Rudolph: "The two cardinal principles of English Puritanism which most profoundly affected the development of New England and the United States were not religious tenets, but educational ideals: a learned clergy and a lettered people."[3] These early institutions were the liberal arts colleges of their day.

Sectarian strife.   It is unfortunate that from the very beginning sectarian struggles hampered the development of the early colleges. Often these struggles attained a virulence and pettiness that seem incredible from a modern point of view. The problem is brilliantly detailed in the modern classic *The Development of Academic Freedom in the United States,*[4] and every person who is interested at all in church-related higher education should regard this book as required reading. Especially ought such a person to read the fifteen

---

[2] John S. Brubacher and Willis Rudy, *Higher Education in Transition* (New York: Harper & Row, Publishers, 1958), p. 6.

[3] C. Frederick Rudolph, *The American College and University* (New York: Alfred A. Knopf, Inc., 1962), p. 6.

[4] Richard Hofstadter and Walter P. Metzger, *The Development of Academic Freedom in the United States* (New York: Columbia University Press, 1955).

pages entitled "Sectarianism at Yale," which the authors term a case study in illiberalism. "There an attempt was made to reduce one of the major colonial colleges to the status of a severely sectarian agency, foreshadowing many of the small church-dominated colleges that were to spring up in such profusion throughout the country in the early nineteenth century." [5] One should beware of reading ancient history in terms of modern standards, thus obtaining a false idea; yet the lesson of those days dare not be regarded as irrelevant today.

Proliferation. The wild spreading of church colleges in the nineteenth century is now history. On the forefront of the westward movement went the church; and where the church went, so also did countless educational institutions, often calling themselves colleges when they were little more than poor secondary schools. Unhappily, prodigality in the founding of colleges was never matched by parallel continuing support. It is no wonder that most of these colleges failed. At least 80 per cent of those founded before the Civil War had ceased to exist by 1932.

There were a number of reasons for this proliferation, but a source of encouragement was the famous Dartmouth College decision of 1819. When it appeared that the legislature of New Hampshire might void the terms of the charter of Dartmouth College, the expansion of colleges had already begun. Had the Dartmouth decision voided the charter, the future of American higher education might have been quite different. The decision meant that charters granted to private colleges could not be abrogated by state legislatures.

Although the schools died for many reasons, financial stringency was the chief one. The nation itself was economically insecure, and when depression struck (as it did again and again, at least locally), the weak institution succumbed. Since there were so many of them, the colleges often entered into ruinous competition with one another, often on purely denominational lines. Many of the institutions were located in out-of-the-way places, at times by design but often by misappraisal of the promise of the region. Thus Beloit College, chartered in 1845, was located 500 miles from a bank, and three-days' drive from the nearest city. Contributions came

---

[5] *Ibid.,* p. 163.

from the town, from eastern men interested in church education, and from regional subscriptions.[6]

There can be no doubt that many small contributions represented genuinely sacrificial giving by men and women of very modest means. That Beloit College has survived and is today an institution of strength and promise is a tribute to many ordinary people who lacked education themselves. It would be ingratitude of the worst sort to forget the fact.

Catastrophic endings were all too common among the small frontier institutions. Fire was a particular danger, and more than one tiny college—often only a single building—went up in smoke to final doom. Cokesbury College, the first attempt at higher education by the Methodists, twice burned to the ground and was then never again revived. Some of the first funds for this ill-starred institution were raised by Bishop Asbury in the ice and snow of Baltimore as part of a house-to-house solicitation for funds. No one ought to question the earnestness of the men who labored for even the most short-lived church college.

The great retrogression. The period of wildest proliferation of church colleges has been termed by Hofstadter and Hardy "The Great Retrogression."[7] The phrase is not too strong. Two major problems are indicated—local pride and denominational zeal—each of which has had long-range implications for American education. They are problems not as yet fully understood by the churches. For instance, one town would bid strenuously against another for a proposed seat of learning, and while the bids were almost never adequate, or even substantial, they were heard. Often two colleges were founded in nearby communities to satisfy both competing towns, when one institution would obviously have been much stronger and could easily have served the whole area. The point would be of little importance were it not that some of the same factors are operative even today.

In 1961 the Presbyterians of North Carolina opened a new college which was the merger of several relatively weak institutions. After exhaustive studies by competent experts, it was decided to found the merged institution at Laurinburg, North Carolina, under

---

[6] George P. Schmidt, *The Liberal Arts College* (New Jersey: Rutgers University Press, 1957).

[7] Hofstadter and Metzger, *op. cit.*, pp. 211 ff.

the name St. Andrews College. A new plant, both imaginative and effective, is being developed. Its orientation and programming are clear-cut and distinctive. In the process of seeking its new site, however, a number of North Carolina communities entered the initial bidding, and two of the disappointed cities offered sizable grants to another denomination to sponsor colleges for them. The offer was accepted in both cases. Now there are three new struggling institutions confronting one another, where one strong college, jointly supported, might be vigorous enough to influence the whole region positively. Two of the new institutions are only forty-three miles apart.

Thus the building of new church colleges, particularly in the South, continues. It should be said, fortunately, that there is increasing cooperation in support of church colleges by Protestant bodies. Roman Catholic colleges too are growing in number, and at a much higher rate than that of Protestant colleges. Most of the new Roman Catholic colleges are being founded in or near large metropolitan areas.

The second problem suggested by Hofstadter and Hardy—denominational zeal—has been solved by history. In an earlier day church colleges were frequently the most violent opponents of new public institutions. Too often the label "godless" was attached to the new public institutions by those who should have known better. Such labeling, while rarely heard today, is unhappily still not completely out of fashion. In some early instances, new public institutions came quickly under the control of boards heavily dominated by men of sectarian interest, particularly in the South.[8] This situation has fortunately been changed by the tide of events. If the church college is to survive, it must now stand on solid educational grounds to interpret its mission. This is not to say, as will appear subsequently, that "educational grounds" are necessarily without religious implications.

Checks upon proliferation. In the founding of new colleges, do church leaders understand the extraordinary financial needs of the institutions they are now too weakly supporting? The answer is that in nearly all churches—both Protestant and Catholic—the locus of decision is usually regional or local, and local groups are

---

[8] John S. Brubacher and Willis Rudy, *Higher Education in Transition* (New York: Harper & Row, Publishers, 1958), pp. 139–44.

thinking in terms of local needs and ambitions. Church bodies in national session may establish principles and guidelines; it is the local governing bodies that to a large degree determine what is to be done.

On this point The Methodist Church may be taken as an illustration. Methodism entered the field of higher education relatively late, but once in the business it created institutions more rapidly than any other Protestant body. It early became apparent to leaders of the strongest Methodist colleges that unwise proliferation was dangerous to the future of every college. As a result of much discussion the General Board of Education of the Methodist Episcopal Church was created in 1868 to aid its educational institutions, especially through a student loan fund. (The Presbyterians had established a Board of Education nearly fifty years earlier.)

In 1892, as a second step, the University Senate of The Methodist Church was created by the General Conference to serve as counselor to the Board of Education. The senate was early given the right of investigation of Methodist educational institutions, but it was a power rarely used. The senate was from the beginning made up of practical educators, that is, men serving actively in educational institutions. Its first order of business at Syracuse University in 1893 was the setting up of standards, both for the measuring of institutions already in existence and for new ones under consideration. It approved a list of institutions considered eligible to participate in the Methodist Student Loan Fund—one of the first lists, if not the very first list, of accreditations published in the United States.

Although valiant efforts were made by the senate and the Board of Education to curb unwise expansion, these agencies were extremely limited in authority, and even today new colleges may be founded without the approval of these bodies. What is true of the Methodists is more or less true of every other church body. Unwise expansion unhappily continues, though at a relatively slow rate among the Protestants, even as long-established institutions suffer for want of funds.

Standards. Inextricably related to the problem of expansion and support is that of quality. Too often religious enthusiasm has been permitted to substitute for academic standards. There were also frequent attacks upon what was early only a vague notion of academic freedom and the right to teach the facts as one saw them.

More than one institution severed its connections with its church because the college could no longer tolerate the attacks which came to it from every side when an orthodoxy was challenged. It was, to be sure, not only the churches which were suspicious of new ideas, but in many instances the attacks from clergymen were particularly virulent. Hofstadter and Metzger make the point well:

> The worst thing that can be said of the sponsors and promoters of the old colleges is not that they failed to foster sufficiently free teaching and research in their own colleges, but that when others attempted to found freer and more advanced institutions the denominational forces tried to cripple or destroy their work. In the contemporary American educational system the great universities and leading colleges call the tune, and even the smaller church-related institutions (the heirs of the old denominational colleges) very often share to some degree their ideas of academic freedom. In the denominational era, the small denominational colleges set the pattern, and even the would-be sponsors of universities were hamstrung by that circumstance.[9]

There are large credits.   What has gone before is history, and as usual in history extravagancies and weaknesses loom large. In looking backward, the debits are apparent. What about the credits?

The credits are by any standard important. Actually the churches deserve gratitude for many generous contributions to American higher education. A few of these follow:

1. Founding of higher education in the New World upon a basis which has proved itself fruitful and which has led to the extraordinary flexibility of American higher education.
2. Spreading of educational opportunity to every corner of the nation.
3. Efforts to relate intelligence to high religious aspiration and to the urgent demand for social reform in a nation in travail.
4. Building of many institutions of exceptional power which, while no longer bearing any legal relationship with a church, still seek to maintain a religious orientation to their work.
5. Development and maintenance today of a substantial group of colleges acknowledging affiliation with the church and supported by the churches.
6. Development of a spirit of individual and group support for independent higher education which has become a pattern for American giving to all types of educational institutions. Countless contri-

---

[9] Hofstadter and Metzger, *op. cit.,* p. 211.

butions from church sources—large and small—were made by men and women who had not themselves enjoyed the benefits of even a secondary education.

7. A steady stream of young men and women educated in church-related colleges and universities, who by their lives have enriched the nation and the world.

These are part, but by no means all, of the contributions of the church to higher education in the United States. If the record is in some ways marred, it parallels closely that of every area of American life. Actually it is the record of human beings trying—often failing, but at times victorious.

CHAPTER II

The Church-Related College Today

Definitions

What is a church-related college? For the purposes of this study, a church-related college is defined as one which lists itself as such in one or more of three major directories—*American Universities and Colleges* (1960), *American Junior Colleges* (1960), and *Education Directory* (1960–61)—or which in *American Universities and Colleges* indicates election or nomination of trustees by church bodies. This definition does not represent the final word on the subject of church relationship, but it is a helpful and objective approach to the problem.

Colleges and universities. There are numerous church-related universities in the United States, but these are not included in this study since they represent a complexity with which it is not possible to deal in a monograph of short scope. There is no precision in the United States in the general use of the term "university." Many small colleges are called universities, but some make no pretensions of being technically such. Some institutions named "colleges" are universities. In this monograph the definition of a university is that devised by the United States Office of Education:

> Institutions which (1) give considerable stress to graduate instruction, (2) confer advanced degrees as well as bachelor's degrees in a variety of liberal arts fields, and (3) have at least two professional schools not exclusively technological.[1]

Arbitrary decisions have therefore been made by the author as to which of the church-related institutions are by this definition universities. In general, if an institution offers the Ph.D. in a number of fields, it has been classified as a university and has been excluded from this study. In addition, seven other institutions which enroll

---

[1] Office of Education, *Statistics of Higher Education, 1957–1958* (Washington, D.C.: Government Printing Office, 1961), p. 119.

more than 3,500 students have been omitted, since these institutions appear atypical.

There are new institutions of higher education which are not listed in any one of the directories mentioned previously, and they are excluded from this study. Among these are colleges which have not yet been accredited by a regional agency. Some of these have had auspicious beginnings while others appear to face severe difficulties.

Excluded also are institutions which train primarily for the Roman Catholic priesthood or for religious communities. Bible colleges represent a special problem and are excluded. These now have their own accrediting agency—The Accrediting Association of Bible Colleges—and define their role thus: "The chief function of Bible colleges is preparing students for Christian ministries." [2]

Enrollments unless otherwise noted will refer to college-grade students registered in the fall of 1959. These are taken directly from the *Education Directory* (1960–61). Total enrollments for the whole year would be considerably higher in every instance. What follows deals therefore with two-, three-, and four-year colleges, some of which offer courses leading to an advanced or first professional degree but not substantial doctoral work in the arts and sciences.

Senior Colleges

There are 528 four-year colleges which meet the specifications for the study. These institutions vary greatly in size and are spread out over 46 states and the District of Columbia.

Enrollments. The facts regarding enrollment are as follows:

SIZES OF THE 528 SENIOR COLLEGES—FALL, 1959

Size Group	Frequency
Below 400	118
400–499	60
500–699	108
700–1000	101
Over 1000	141
Smallest	25
Median	663
Largest	3190

[2] *School and Society* (May 6, 1961), p. 219.

Denominational affiliation. By denominational support the 528 colleges divide as follows in order of frequency of relationship:

DENOMINATIONAL AFFILIATIONS

Roman Catholic	196
Methodist	69
Presbyterian	56
Baptist	35
Lutheran	29
Southern Baptist	20
Disciples of Christ	13
Congregational	12
Society of Friends	10
Seventh Day Adventist	9
Protestant Episcopal	8
Nazarene	6
Church of Christ	5
Evangelical United Brethren	5
Christian Methodist Episcopal	5
African Methodist Episcopal	5
Mennonite	5
Church of Brethren	5
United Presbyterian	5
Evangelical and Reformed	4
United Church of Christ	4
Free Methodist	4
American Missionary Association	3
Brethren	3
Wesleyan Methodist	3
Reformed	2
Moravian	2
Church of God	2
Interdenominational	2
United Brethren	2
Brethren in Christ	2
Reformed Presbyterian	1
Cumberland Presbyterian	1
Church of New Jerusalem	1
United Missionary	1
Christian Reformed	1
Jewish	1
Reorganized Latter Day Saints	1
Adventist Christian	1
United Christian Missionary Society	1
African Methodist Episcopal Zion	1
United Evangelical Lutheran	1
Seventh Day Baptist	1

Since some senior institutions are sponsored by more than one denomination, the total exceeds 528. *The affiliations are as listed by the institutions themselves.*

Accreditation. A preliminary indication of institutional quality is to be found in the accredited status of a college. No assumption is made here that accreditation implies any more than minimal quality, yet it is clear that if a college long in existence cannot achieve accreditation it must have fundamental weaknesses. In the relatively new institution, the lack of accreditation may not be significant, for the regional agencies normally wait until one class has been graduated before seriously considering approval.

Of the 528 colleges, 49 were unaccredited in the fall of 1962. This means that approximately 9 per cent of all church-related senior colleges have not realized this minimal hallmark of quality.

There is a very close correlation between the size of the institution and approval by a regional agency. The following chart documents the point:

ACCREDITATION AS RELATED TO INSTITUTIONAL SIZE

Enrollment Range	Accredited	Unaccredited	Per Cent Accredited
Below 200	15	22	41
200–399	86	12	88
400–599	89	10	90
600–799	95	5	95
Over 800	194	0	100
	479	49	91

The figures represent, in part, a vicious circle. Unaccredited colleges have trouble recruiting adequate student bodies; schools lack the strength they need to become accredited when they cannot enroll an adequate number of students.

The 9 per cent unaccredited institutions represent a severe challenge to this group of institutions. But the problem has other facets. The best of the church-related colleges, for example, though in many instances proud of their denominational affiliation, are fearful of being paired in the minds of the public and of educators with institutions which have not even achieved this minimum level of respectability.

Two-Year Colleges

There are 137 two-year colleges which meet the specifications set for inclusion in the present study. These institutions are spread over 34 states and the District of Columbia.

Enrollment. The church-related two-year colleges are much

more homogeneous in size than are the senior colleges. The figures follow:

ENROLLMENTS IN THE 137 TWO-YEAR COLLEGES

Size Group	Frequency
Below 100	27
100–199	46
200–299	28
300–499	20
500–699	9
700–1,000	5
Over 1,000	2
	137

Smallest	18
Median	185
Largest	1,094

Denominational affiliation. The 137 junior colleges are related to the following denominations in order of frequency of relationship:

DENOMINATIONAL AFFILIATIONS

Roman Catholic	31
Methodist	20
Southern Baptist	17
Baptist	11
Lutheran	11
Presbyterian	11
African Methodist Episcopal	5
Protestant Episcopal	4
Disciples of Christ	3
Free Methodist	3
Evangelical Lutheran	2
Latter Day Saints	2
Mennonite	2
American Baptist	1
American Evangelical Lutheran	1
Church of New Jerusalem	1
Christian Reformed	1
Congregational Christian	1
Evangelical United Brethren	1
Free Will Baptist	1
Mississippi Negro Baptist	1
Moravian	1
Pentecostal Holiness	1
Primitive Baptist	1
Reformed	1
Reorganized Church of Jesus Christ of Latter Day Saints	1
Seventh Day Adventist	1
Wesleyan Methodist	1
	137

Accreditation. Large numbers of the two-year church-related colleges are regionally unaccredited—actually 54 of the total list of 137. By size the unaccredited two-year colleges break down as follows:

UNACCREDITED TWO-YEAR COLLEGES

Enrollment Range	Frequency	Number Unaccredited	Per Cent Unaccredited
Fewer than 100	27	23	85
100–199	46	25	54
200–299	28	6	21
300–499	20	0	0
500–699	9	0	0
700–1,000	5	0	0
Over 1,000	2	0	0
	137	54	39

The 39 per cent of the two-year colleges that are unaccredited are heavily concentrated in the groups with small enrollments.

Enrollments

Enrollments in the 528 four-year colleges were in the fall of 1961 at a high level of 423,195. Of this number 182,869 students, or about 43 per cent, were in the 100 largest institutions (ranging from 1,200 to 3,500). In the 137 junior colleges there were enrolled in the 1961 fall term 33,778 students. The total enrollment for the fall term in the entire group of 665 institutions was 456,973.

For the fall of 1961, the U. S. Office of Education reported 3,891,000 degree-credit enrollments in American institutions of higher education. For purposes of comparative emphasis only, it may be noted that about 11.0 per cent of this total fall enrollment were registered in the institutions here under study.

Selected Institutional Profiles

The statistics which have been presented should help to indicate the extent of the church-college movement in the present day. It is, however, only in the individual situation that one can understand what is going on in American education. In this section a number of institutional profiles are drawn, though not in detail, to illustrate the diversity among the colleges of the group under study. The profiles were selected at random but from various size groups.

Institution A, in a city of some 70,000, is a coeducational college of arts and sciences in Pennsylvania. Sponsored by the Moravian Church in America, it began as a woman's college in 1742, but by 1934 included a school of theology and had become coeducational. Governed by a board of 37, of which all but nine are elected by church groups, the college is accredited by the Middle States Association.

In 1958–59 the college enrolled 794 students of whom approximately 70 per cent were men. In 1950, about 15 per cent of the entering students were from the upper fifth of their high school classes. In 1960, 50 per cent were from the upper fifth and only 3 per cent from the lowest two-fifths. The institution requires College Entrance Examination Board tests of all applicants for admission. The faculty-student ratio in 1960 was about 1 to 15, and about 40 per cent of the faculty held Ph.D. degrees. Book value of the endowment in 1960 was $1,700,000, or slightly in excess of $2,000 per student. The library collection numbered some 50,000 volumes.

Institution B, in a large metropolitan area of Massachusetts, is a college for men and is conducted by the Society of Jesus (Jesuits). The college was founded in 1843. Property is held by a board of six members of the Society elected for one-year terms, but the college is governed by the president under the Provincial of the Order. In 1958–59 the college enrolled 1,823 students, seven of whom were doing graduate work.

College Entrance Examination Board tests are required of all applicants for admission as students, including three scholastic aptitude tests: in English composition, in one modern foreign language studied two years, and in one optional field. Mean scores of admitted students exceeded 600 on both the verbal and mathematical sections of the tests. The college is mainly residential, with more than 80 per cent of all students living on campus.

The college has a library of nearly 200,000 volumes and a faculty of 131, of which not quite 30 per cent hold the doctorate. The institutional endowment is very low, but the plant on a campus of 163 acres is valued at more than $10,000,000.

Institution C, in a town of 2,578 population, is an unaccredited liberal arts college in West Virginia, sponsored by the Seventh Day

Baptist Church. The president defines the institution as "church-related but not church supported." The institution is governed by a board of 36, all of whom are elected by the "stockholders."

In 1960–61 the college enrolled 486 students, about half of whom lived on the campus. Nearly 55 per cent of the total enrollment came from West Virginia and 20 per cent from Pennsylvania. Seventeen states were represented in the student body. While the college uses the School and College Aptitude Test for all entering freshmen, the results are not available.

Endowment is almost negligible and the plant is valued at somewhat less than $500,000. The library collection in 1961 was 21,721 volumes, or approximately 45 books per student. The faculty numbered 33, for a faculty-student ratio of about 1 to 15. The institution has just completed a self-study and has had the benefit of a development study by a national firm of business consultants.

Institution D, in a large metropolitan area, is a coeducational senior college in central Ohio affiliated with the American Lutheran Church. Founded in 1831, it is governed by a board of regents numbering 18, of which 9 are pastors, 6 are laymen, and 3 are women.

The institution enrolled in 1960–61 a total of 1,343, of whom 840 were resident on the campus. Men and women students are about equal in number. Entering freshmen in the fall of 1961 had a median score on the Ohio State Psychological Examination in the sixty-first percentile, and on the American College Test at the sixty-ninth percentile.

The faculty in 1961–62 numbered 72, of whom about 25 per cent held the doctorate. The faculty-student ratio was approximately 1 to 18. The library contained more than 95,000 volumes. The book value of the endowment in 1958–59 was $1,027,187, or about $750 per student. The plant was valued at nearly $7,000,000.

Institution E, in a city of 18,429 in California, is a coeducational college of arts and sciences affiliated with the American Baptist Convention. Founded in 1909, it is governed by a board of 31, of whom the majority are members of the American Baptist Church.

Enrollment in 1958–59 was 1,385 with a few more men than women. All entering students are required to take College Entrance Examination Tests. Almost 90 per cent of the students live on campus.

The faculty in 1958–59 numbered 92, producing a faculty-student ratio of about 1 to 15. Well over 50 per cent of the faculty held the doctorate. The library contained more than 120,000 volumes. Market value of endowment, on the campus of 135 acres, was nearly $6,000,000, and plant value was estimated at about the same figure.

Institution F, in a small city of 15,322 in South Carolina, is a college sponsored by the Methodist Church and attended primarily by Negroes. Founded in 1869, it only recently gained accreditation by the regional agency. It is governed by a board of 21, nominated by the related church body.

Tuition charges were in 1960–61 over $250 per year. It enrolled in 1958–59 a total of 341 students, almost equally divided between men and women. Admission standards require only high school graduation. Ninety per cent of the students live on campus. Book value of the endowment in 1958–59 was $431,000 or $1,264 per student. The plant covers 21 acres and is valued at about $1,000,-000. The library has 16,536 volumes. The faculty numbers 27, of whom about 30 per cent hold the doctorate.

Institution G, in a city of 45,000 in Indiana, is affiliated with the Society of Friends, and has been operating since 1847. All its trustees must be members of the Society of Friends.

The college is coeducational and in 1958–59 enrolled 839, of whom 445 were men. College Entrance Examination Board tests are required. The institution in 1960–61 entered a three-course three-term plan. Nearly 80 per cent of the students live on campus.

Book value of endowment in 1958–59 was $2,275,589. The plant was valued in excess of $5,000,000. The faculty numbered 66, of whom more than 50 per cent held the doctorate. The library contained nearly 100,000 volumes.

Summary

The previous exhibits represent something of the diversity of the institutions under study. These colleges have much in common, yet they also differ greatly. While no junior colleges were included in the preliminary exhibits, those institutions show the same variety as the four-year colleges.

CHAPTER III

Control and Organization

In general, church-related colleges, like other types of colleges and universities in the nation, operate under the control of lay boards of trustees. Although there are many names for these boards other than trustees (i.e., regents, directors, visitors, etc.), the variety of names does not indicate any differences in function. Here they will be referred to as boards of trustees, whatever their titles. By "lay trustee" is meant an educational layman. A major exception to lay government is to be found among Roman Catholic colleges.

An overview. An analysis of boards of trustees of American colleges and universities was made by Walter Crosby Eells in 1961.[1] Eells was dealing only with senior colleges and universities listed in the 1960 edition of *American Universities and Colleges,* hence only with accredited institutions. He noted great diversity in the names of the boards of control, in their methods of selection, number of members, terms of office, and other features. The same diversity appears among church-related colleges.

Most Protestant church-related institutions have a majority of trustees either elected or approved by the supporting denominational body. The Eells study indicates that the size of governing boards varies greatly, from well over 100 to as few as three. The same variations are to be found among boards of church colleges.

Boards of public institutions tend to be much smaller than those of private institutions, with a median of 10 for public institutions as compared to a median of 24 for private schools and colleges. Here again, however, there is a substantial variation between institutions of the Roman Catholic Church, for which the median is seven, to Methodist and Baptist boards, for which the median is 32. Terms of office of trustees vary too, from 16 years for board members of

---

[1] Walter Crosby Eells, "Boards of Control of Universities and Colleges," *The Educational Record* (October, 1961), pp. 336–42. This study deals with both public and private institutions.

the University of California and 14 years for trustees of Louisiana State University to terms of only one year in a few colleges.

Boards of Control of Roman Catholic Institutions

Catholic institutions for the most part have boards of trustees which deal with legal matters, especially the holding of property. Most commonly these are chosen from members of the staff of the college itself. They do not normally control educational policies or select the executive officers of the institution. It is in the selection of the president that Catholic boards differ most notably from their Protestant counterparts. Only rarely is the president of a Catholic college a layman. Again in the Catholic institution the property of the college or university is held by the board of trustees for the sponsoring religious community.

Many Catholic colleges have been very successful in creating voluntary bodies to serve as counselors and consultants to the administration in a variety of ways. Nevertheless, it has been said that "Those powers, which in other types of institutions are exercised by the boards of trustees, are in the Catholic institutions lodged in the ecclesiastical hierarchy or in the religious orders under whose auspices the institutions are operated." [2]

Protestant Boards of Control

There is a wide diversity among Protestant colleges in their relationships to the sponsoring churches. Surely it must be said that the church does not always fully understand the educational problems confronting the institutions it supports. Often the college is not completely sure what church affiliation means, a question that ought to be high on the agenda of every church college.

In the large majority of Protestant institutions in the group under study here, college property is not technically "owned" by the church itself. It is held by the board of trustees of the college. There

---

[2] Mary Irwin, ed., *American Universities and Colleges* (Washington, D.C.: American Council on Education, 1960), p. 19.

are, nevertheless, numerous institutions actually "owned" by the sponsoring church, though even in these cases it is understood that the property of the college is held in trust "for" the sponsoring church.

In a recent clarification of relationships between the Methodist Church and one of the colleges related to it, the charter was so amended as to place institutional property in the hands of the board of trustees, but with a reversionary clause that would enable the Methodist Board of Education, a national agency, to reclaim the property for the church should the institution ever be adjudged as out of sympathy with the educational ideals of the church. It is scarcely conceivable, however, that the powers of such a clause should ever be invoked.

In general, church bodies influence college direction by the right to elect, nominate, or approve members of the governing board of the institution. What the situation is at this point may be illustrated by the following table which represents a random sampling of the makeup of twenty-one governing boards of church-related colleges. In this listing only senior colleges are included, but among the number are both accredited and unaccredited institutions (which was not the case in the Eells study referred to previously). While the governing boards of church-related junior colleges tend to be smaller than those of the four-year institutions, there are no other major deviations.

From this sampling it may be seen that there is considerable variation in the proportion of the board named by a church body. Yet there is a growing tendency among churches to allow the board to name trustees at large, so as to assure a wider geographical spread and to permit elections by alumni.

Board structure. A random sampling (over 10 per cent) of all the senior colleges studied indicates that more than one-fourth of the group include alumni representatives. Approximately 10 per cent of the sampling required that a majority of members be affiliated with the sponsoring church, with a few requiring that at least three-fourths be members of the sponsoring church. No Protestant institution in the group required that all trustees be members of the affiliated church or even Protestants. In nearly one-fourth of the

CHURCH REPRESENTATION ON SENIOR COLLEGE GOVERNING BOARDS–SAMPLING

Institution	Denomination	Size of Board	Number of Members Elected, Nominated, or Approved by Church
1	Methodist	25	25
2	Methodist	30	22
3	Congregational	15	0
4	Southern Baptist	25	25
5	Brethren	29	15
6	Seventh Day Adventist	16	16
7	Baptist	31	21
8	Lutheran	26	26
9	Methodist	40	21
10	Lutheran	24	24
11	Congregational-Methodist	17	12
12	Christian Reformed	40	40
13	Lutheran	21	12
14	Episcopal	115	105
15	Presbyterian	26	18
16	Baptist	36	0
17	Church of God	24	16
18	Evangelical Reformed	37	20
19	Friends	24	0
20	Baptist	44	22
21	Southern Baptist	39	39

sampling, college presidents were themselves members of the board of trustees.

A differentiation must be made between election of trustees by the ecclesiastical body and nomination or approval by such a body. The data at hand were not sufficient to make any useful judgments as to whether or not election by church bodies usually involves prior consultation either with the board itself or with the college president. It is the impression of the author that election and nomination most frequently follow suggestions by the college president. In times of stress, nevertheless, the right to elect without consultation may represent a strong control by the sponsoring church; but in many instances approval by church bodies is largely automatic so long as conditions of the college charter and bylaws are fulfilled.

One substantial institution has a joint board of 36 trustees and 12 visitors. In normal operations the board and visitors operate as a unit, but in the election of a president the visitors, all elected by the sponsoring church, are solely responsible for initiating nominations. In another urban institution all trustee nominations are made to the sponsoring church by the executive committee of the board.

A strong college related to the Protestant Episcopal Church lists a board of trustees of 115, including six alumni and four members of the faculty. Forty-two are laymen and the others, excepting faculty and alumni representatives, are clergymen. In this institution, however, there is a board of regents elected by the board of trustees, of whom three are bishops, three clergymen, six laymen, plus the chancellor and vice chancellor. The regents serve as the executive body of the entire board.

In general the trend is toward a smaller percentage of clergymen on the board, though in some denominations clergymen are still in the majority on the boards of their colleges. The need for financial understanding and support has tended to increase the number of laymen, as has the general principle promulgated by the regional agencies that a variety of vocational and professional groups should be represented on the board. A recommendation that not more than one-third of the board should represent a single profession was adopted in 1935 by the North Central Association of Colleges and Secondary Schools and probably has had much to do with this shift.

Although the board is legally responsible for policy-making, there is a growing understanding among trustees that educational policies should be formulated by the faculty and that actual administration of the college should not be a board function. There are still, unhappily, glaring violations of this principle. Even so, trustees are learning that the financial implications of educational policy and practice cannot be ignored, though at present there is little general agreement as to how the board may take a more active role in educational matters without intruding upon areas beyond their competence.

Organization and Administration

The organizational structure of the church-related college parallels closely that of other types of institutions of similar size and function. Again the decisive factor is size. A more or less characteristic organization chart of top administrative officers is shown in Figure 1. Local situations vary, and the historical context in which the administration finds itself at the moment will have much to do with specific assignments to various offices. In general, however, the pattern charted in Figure 1 is becoming more common.

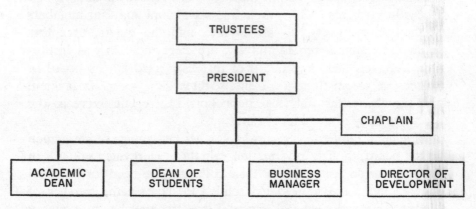

Figure 1. Typical Organizational Chart

Unit control is almost universally recognized as essential to the successful management of an educational institution. Thus, only the president is normally held directly responsible to the board of trustees. His major officers are the dean of the college, the dean of students, the business manager, and the director of development. There is a variety of titles for each of these officials. A growing tendency is to name one or several of these officers "vice president," for reasons which hardly seem cogent in a small institution. Years ago, nearly every church-related college had a vice president whose function was commonly to arrange and preside at chapel and to countersign checks in the absence of the president. This functionary is disappearing.

Today the director of development is frequently a vice president, on the perhaps dubious theory that he requires such a title to speak more effectively for the president to important potential donors. By almost inevitable but strained logic some academic deans have been named vice presidents so that the academic function of the college would not appear subservient to that of financial development. In other cases, the business manager, having outlasted numerous presidents, was honored for long service by being named a vice president; and again the academic dean could not be slighted without supposed damage to the academic emphasis. Yet the title of dean has a long and honorable history. There appears very little merit in multiplying vice presidents in smaller institutions, for whatever reasons, yet the process goes on.

The larger the college, the more likely it is to have two, three, or even four vice presidents, each mainly responsible for the functions listed under other titles in Figure 1. In many colleges there is still no dean of students but rather a dean of men and a dean of women. As smaller institutions add the office of dean of students, this official may also for a time be dean of men.

In the more sophisticated institutions the president has limited his span of control as indicated in the illustrative organizational chart; yet in numerous colleges as many as a dozen or more officers still report directly to the president. Increasingly, registrars report to academic deans or to deans of students, and admissions officers report to one or the other of the deans, depending upon the administrative philosophy of the president. Librarians continue to report directly to the president in the smaller colleges, but there is a strong tendency for the librarian to be responsible to the academic dean.

Increasingly, college presidents prepare their annual, and at times semi-annual, reports to the board well in advance of the board meetings so that trustees can study them before the meetings. In some colleges the president will include with his report to the trustees careful reports to him from his chief line-officers. In other cases the president uses the reports of his staff in his own statement to the board.

A growing tendency is for presidents to invite to board meetings, upon concurrence of the board, his chief officers so that they may come to appreciate the total concerns of the governing board. As a rule, these officers do not speak in board meetings unless called upon and do not vote. The board may at any time go into executive session and exclude all but trustees.[3]

There is a great variation in the complexity of organization of church-related colleges. One Protestant institution enrolling over 2,000 students, for example, employs a full-time student personnel staff of five in addition to eight paid house counselors. None of these

---

[3] While the practice of inviting chief officers to board meetings is growing, there is still debate as to whether or not such procedure constitutes a violation of the unit control principle. A brief but systematic treatment of the point is to be found in David G. Mobberley and Myron F. Wicke, *The Deanship of the Liberal Arts College* (Nashville, Tenn.: Methodist Board of Education, 1962), pp. 26–27.

teach at all, nor are they members of the faculty. Another Protestant institution of considerable strength, enrolling 700 students, has a part-time dean of men, a part-time dean of women, a part-time director of testing and guidance, and in each dormitory a matron without professional training of any kind. In the same institution the dean serves also as registrar, though the actual day-to-day functioning of the registrar's office is in the hands of a recorder with a staff of two full-time assistants. In many colleges the chaplain is directly responsible to the president regarding his pastoral functions but to the dean regarding his teaching functions, if any.

The key to many problems in academic administration of church-colleges is the nature of the presidency and the character of the president. For many years most presidents were clergymen, and all studies suggest that a substantial majority of presidents of church-related colleges still are clergymen today. A study of administrators of Methodist educational institutions in 1961 found that only 32 of 74 senior college presidents were laymen. The more conservative the denomination, however, the more likely the president is to be a clergyman.

Small, impecunious colleges are subject to the most self-defeating types of one-man rule. A president may choose to make all decisions himself, even though his organization appears on paper to make room for participation in decision-making. Too many church-related colleges are operated as though the institution had to be preserved at any cost, regardless of its influence upon individuals and society. From long observation, the author concludes that, as faculties grow more effective and distinguished, they demand more self-government and will submit less and less to autocratic rule.

Trustee boards tend to follow the recommendations of the president they have elected. Trustees normally concern themselves first with budgets; and when these are in balance, they too often ask no further questions. Trustees ought, however, to assure themselves first of all that the budget has not been balanced at the expense of educational quality. This is often a special danger in a group of institutions that are small and inadequately financed, though operating upon what may appear to be high motives. Among the institutions under study there are outstanding administrations, yet there are too many that are shoddy and indefensible.

CHAPTER IV

Purposes of Church Colleges

The question of purpose is always fundamental in education. It is a particularly difficult question for colleges and universities because of the so-called explosion of knowledge. Educators too often operate upon the basis of cliches and slogans, and too rarely are purposes examined in depth.

Protagonists of church colleges very easily fall victim to cliches, perhaps because the ends they seek appear so laudable. Nevertheless many critics are suspicious of such avowed goals as "education for character," and the skepticism is justified. Is "education for character" achievable by the means proposed by church colleges, or even achievable at all? It should be added at once that these institutions are not alone in their too bland assurance that an ideal once stated is thereby achieved. Many verbal educational stereotypes are never examined. Thus the popular "search for truth" may produce little more than new piles of facts which too often have been developed only to prove that someone with a conflicting idea is in error. All educational institutions should examine their purposes with modesty and skepticism.

Nevertheless the church-related colleges, at least as a group, have not adequately kept their purposes clear. Often the institutions appear to be seeking support for what vigorous though sympathetic critics deem poor reasons, neglecting thereby the inherent potentialities of their own mission.

Early Studies of Purpose

The bibliography dealing with the purposes of church-related colleges is a large and growing one. Here only a few of the more significant documents will be referred to.

The following careful studies of Protestant denominational efforts in higher education appeared several decades ago, between 1929 and 1932. Each of the three has its especial merits:

29

Leonard, R. J., *et al.*, *Survey of Higher Education for the United Lutheran Church in America*, 2 vols. (New York: Teachers College, Columbia University, 1929). A general picture and evaluation of the educational work of the United Lutheran Church with particular reference to higher education.

Reeves, Floyd W. and John Dale Russell, *College Organization and Administration* (Indianapolis, Ind.: Board of Education, Disciples of Christ, 1929). Drawn chiefly from surveys made of sixteen colleges and universities affiliated with the Board of Education of The Disciples of Christ.

Reeves, Floyd W., *et al.*, *The Liberal Arts College* (Chicago: University of Chicago Press, 1932). Based upon surveys of thirty-five colleges related to the Methodist Episcopal Church.

The most complete summary of stated aims of a group of church-related colleges appears in *The Liberal Arts College*.[1] The major aims, in order of frequency among 33 colleges, follow:

Aims	*Frequency*
Development of Christian character	26
Development of scholarly attitudes and habits	19
Vocational training	10
Broad, liberal, cultural education	9
Professional training	8
Training for citizenship	7

The surveyors noted that too few of the institutions had actually given serious thought to their purposes, and in many instances the authors found the stated aims to be clearly in conflict with college practices.

In 1940 there appeared a comprehensive examination of the purposes of the college.[2] The study, by Leslie K. Patton, involved some 260 church-related liberal arts colleges which in 1940 enrolled fewer than 600 students. In addition 52 independent colleges of comparable size were included as a check group. Among the church colleges were 198 Protestant and 62 Catholic institutions.

Patton used as a definition of the church-related college an adaptation of that developed by the Carnegie Foundation for the Advancement of Teaching.[3] The Patton definition was this: "A

---

[1] Floyd W. Reeves, *et al.*, *The Liberal Arts College* (Chicago: University of Chicago Press, 1932).

[2] Leslie K. Patton, *The Purposes of Church-Related Colleges* (New York: Teachers College, Columbia University, 1940).

[3] *First Annual Report of the President and Treasurer* (New York: Carnegie Foundation for the Advancement of Teaching, 1960), p. 48.

church-related college is an institution which has a definite relationship, either legal, affiliated, or sympathetic, to an established religious body or to some unit of such a body." [4]

Patton read catalog statements for 1933, 1934, and 1937. In addition he sent out 246 questionnaires from which he received nearly 75 per cent response. Along with the questionnaires came numerous letters from college presidents elaborating on the questionnaire responses.

The following summary suggests the major aims of 100 of the colleges which gave either catalog data or presidents' replies:

[4] Patton, op. cit., p. 17.

PERCENTAGE OF ONE HUNDRED COLLEGES STATING MAJOR PURPOSES
IN 1937–38 *

STATED PURPOSE	CATALOG	PRESIDENTS' REPLIES	ONE OR OTHER
A. *Character Development; Ethical Relations*			
1. Development of Christian character	74	71	90
2. Moral training; ethical relations	28	17	38
3. Christian faculty chosen	12	16	24
4. Educate lay and professional church leaders	20	28	38
5. Church attendance required	11	0	11
6. Many rules against misconduct	9	1	9
One or more purposes in Group A	83	83	95
B. *Liberal, Cultural Education*			
7. Provide liberal, cultural education	53	46	77
8. Emphasize high scholarship; independent study	22	9	27
9. Help student integrate knowledge	8	2	9
One or more purposes in Group B	61	52	83
C. *Mental Development*			
10. How to think, training in	16	15	27
11. Tools of knowledge, use of	2	3	4
12. Mental discipline	1	7	8
One or more purposes in Group C	19	23	35
D. *Citizenship, Social Responsibility*			
13. Citizenship, social responsibility	33	38	56
14. Foster student self-government	7	8	12
15. Social, community leadership	18	31	40
16. Understand economic, social order	14	11	23
One or more purposes in Group D	43	52	65

* Rarely checked items are omitted and the numbering is therefore changed from the original.

STATED PURPOSE	CATALOG	PRESIDENTS' REPLIES	ONE OR OTHER
E. *Attention to the Individual*			
17. Manners, social adjustments	19	16	31
18. Good faculty-student relations	10	5	14
19. Individual's needs, attention to	13	17	27
20. Self-help; aid needy students	11	2	12
21. Self-mastery; mental health	10	6	15
22. Government parental; strict discipline	4	0	4
One or more purposes in Group E	45	32	63
F. *Vocational Interests*			
23. Graduate work preparation; pre-professional	36	31	57
24. Vocational training, preparation	17	26	40
25. Teacher training	21	22	35
26. Choice of vocation, aid in			
27. Ministry, preparatory training for	13	5	17
One or more purposes in Group F	49	52	75
G. *Avocational and Extracurricular Activities*			
28. Extracurricular activities, encourage participation	26	21	41
29. Beauty, art—enjoy and create	23	20	35
30. Leisure, worthy use of	5	7	10
One or more purposes in Group G	39	34	57
H. *Curricular Emphases*			
31. Physical health, athletics	41	33	59
32. Home, marriage, parenthood	6	13	15
33. Speech, emphasize importance of	7	2	8

Patton's analysis resulted in his summary of "six significant aspects." Among these were the following: [5]

> Most of the colleges do not emphasize their church relationship. In fact, many of them take great pains to stress their nonsectarian policies and practices. It is noteworthy that in many cases (there was) a full statement of institutional purposes in campaign material for raising funds. If an explicit statement of aims and purposes of the college is an asset in a fund-raising campaign (a critical test when the campaigner needs to make clear the unique function of the institution), then it should be an asset in the maintenance and improvement of the institution during normal times. It is commendable that some of the statements of purpose submitted by the college executives included ways and means of implementing the aims.

---

[5] Patton, *op. cit.*, pp. 97–98.

Sampling of Current Statements of Purpose

In the years between 1940, when the Patton study was made, and 1962, great changes have occurred. Enrollments have soared, and a 600 maximum enrollment for this group of colleges no longer applies. The *median* enrollment of the senior colleges under study here is 663, higher by 63 than the *maximum* of the Patton study.

What do official church-related college statements affirm as major purposes today? Given below are five published statements, somewhat abbreviated, which appear to the author to represent the various approaches now being made to the problem.

Institution A. This is a four-year Protestant college in the Midwest. In the fall of 1961 it enrolled 1,377 students. It has a long tradition of academic excellence and has a chapter of Phi Beta Kappa. The following statement of purpose was developed jointly by faculty, administration, and trustees:

A. To preserve and enrich the cultural and spiritual heritage from which the college grew.

B. To provide a four-year liberal education that serves to guide personal growth, future study, and useful occupation. Such an effort embraces:

    1. An imagination cultivated to conceive possible new developments in understanding and facility in the acquisition and critical assimilation of facts about nature and human society.

    2. Familiarity with the major ideas that have molded history and which pervade present culture and its institutions.

    3. Competence in discerning principles that order knowledge and permit conclusions supported by valid evidence.

    4. Sensitivity to and responsibility for developing major aesthetic, social, moral, and religious values nourished by a Christian view of the world and man's place in it.

    5. Competence in oral and written communications in English and in at least one foreign language.

    6. Desire for and skill in the process of learning as a lifetime enterprise which insures resourcefulness in vocations and satisfactions in avocations.

    7. A sense of destiny to contribute to each generation through work that increases enduring human values.

C. To provide a community of learning on a small residential campus where students and professors by direct association search for the ideas that structure civilization and for the ideals that will enrich it.

D. To provide educational opportunities for students from a cross section of economic groups, social classes, and geographical areas without distinction of race or creed.

E. To supply the fundamentals of all higher education with a view to competence and Christian service in vocations and professions.

Institution B. This is a liberal arts college for women in New England, founded and conducted by the Catholic Sisters of Saint Anne. Accredited regionally, the college enrolled 350 students in 1960. The statement of purpose was developed by the president and the dean in 1955.

College B is a Catholic liberal arts college, where the ideals of a Catholic education inspire and permeate all the objectives of the traditional liberal arts.

The liberal arts are those disciplines which provide the human intellect and will with the most complete training. Although traditionally restricted to a well-defined curriculum, the liberal arts are the results of a method of instruction rather than of definite subject matter.

In agreement with this principle, the teaching in all the departments (of the college) aims at developing specific qualities of the intellect and habits of the will. Thus, the basic subjects taught during the student's first two years at college are planned to train the mind in precision, objectivity, and perspective and to favor the arts of appreciation and expression. The work of the last two years is designed to produce depth and integration, while at the same time taking into consideration the individual needs, talents, and interests of each student. Indeed, it is a constant preoccupation at College B to adapt the choice of courses to the student, with due respect for her personality and potentialities.

In the junior and senior years, the students concentrate in a subject of their choice. This field of concentration, it is felt, is the framework on which a unified structure can be built. The integrating influence of philosophy is revealed to each student in the field of particular interest to her because it is only through depth of study that she becomes conscious of problems whose solution is found in the application of the abstract principles of philosophical speculation. This specialization also prepares the students for a definite area of useful and remunerative activity.

As a Catholic institution of liberal arts, College B reserves a central place to the study of theology which, it is hoped, will direct the students in the elaboration and practice of supernatural ideals. Although the explicit exposition of theological principles is reserved to a few hours each week, theological thinking is never foreign to any subject. The atmosphere is decidedly Catholic at all times. In this environment, the students can develop the habit of truly Christ-like living. Residence at the College provides facilities for daily attendance at Mass and the frequent reception of the Sacraments.

The student's disciplinary life is ordained to promote the free exercise of the will through the voluntary observance of college regulations, through cooperation with the members of the faculty, and through the formation of habits of self-control. The student is trained to be a leader, to take the initiative, to employ leisure hours in constructive effort, to assume a generous share of responsibility in the various college functions, to shun all social codes at variance with Catholic principles. Thus, she gives her student life a maximum of fruitfulness and prepares for an enlightened Catholic leadership in social circles and in the families of tomorrow.

Institution C. This is an interdenominational liberal arts college in the Midwest enrolling in 1961 nearly 2,000 students. The college has been regionally accredited since 1916. The published statement of purpose is followed by a note on "implementation." Added here also, because of its relevance to the question of purpose, is a "Statement of Faith" which must be reaffirmed annually by all faculty and staff.

Purposes of College C

1. To provide a liberal education that introduces the student to the organized fields of learning and presents the Christian theistic view of the world, of man, and of man's culture in the light of Biblical and natural revelation.

2. To enable the student to understand truth in his study of Scripture, of nature, and of man; to pursue righteousness in the individual life and in society; and to appreciate beauty both in God's creation and in human literature and the arts.

3. To assist the student to understand, respect, and evaluate the thoughts of others and to express his own thoughts clearly and effectively.

4. To provide opportunity for concentration and research in one field of learning and to lay the foundation for graduate and professional training.

5. To help the student understand the meaning of life and his role in society and the church, and to prepare him for the responsible use of his freedom and ability by virtue of his commitment to Jesus Christ as Savior and Lord.

6. To aid the student in developing habits which will contribute to his well-being—physical, psychological, and spiritual—and will enable him to participate constructively in community and church life.

Implementation

Because the Scriptures are the integrating core for a Christian liberal arts education, each student takes courses in Bible, Christian doctrine and apologetics, so that he may understand more fully the bearing of the Christian faith on life and thought.

The College endeavors to maintain the highest academic standards by encouraging faculty excellence both in teaching and in scholarship, and by encouraging students in independent study, analytic thinking and the quest for excellence.

Numerous opportunities are provided for cultural enrichment, social development, and athletic endeavor.

As a liberal arts institution which lays the foundation for graduate and professional training, the College helps prepare students for the ministry, education, medicine, science and technology, law, government service, and business, as well as various scholarly fields.

Although primarily a liberal arts college, this institution offers professional training in such fields as education, nursing, and music. The Graduate School offers specialized studies in various areas of theology, in preparation for the ministry, teaching, and missions.

Statement of Faith

(Required of all Faculty Members)

We believe in the Scriptures of the Old and the New Testaments as verbally inspired by God and inerrant in the original writing, and that they are of supreme and final authority in faith and life.

We believe in one God, eternally existing in three persons: Father, Son, and Holy Spirit.

We believe that Jesus Christ was begotten by the Holy Spirit, born of the Virgin Mary, and is true God and true man.

We believe that man was created in the image of God; that he sinned, and thereby incurred not only physical death, but also that spiritual death which is separation from God; and that all human beings are born with a sinful nature, and, in the case of those who reach moral responsibility, become sinners in thought, word and deed.

We believe that the Lord Jesus Christ died for our sins, according to the Scriptures, as a representative and substitutionary sacrifice; and that all who believe in Him are justified on the ground of His shed blood.

We believe in the resurrection of the crucified body of our Lord, in His ascension into Heaven, and in His present life there for us, as High Priest and Advocate.

We believe in "that blessed hope," the personal premillennial, and imminent return of our Lord and Saviour, Jesus Christ.

We believe that all who receive by faith the Lord Jesus Christ are born again of the Holy Spirit, and thereby become children of God.

We believe in the bodily resurrection of the just and the unjust, the everlasting blessedness of the saved, and the everlasting punishment of the lost.

Institution D.   This is a coeducational institution in the South related to one of the smaller, more conservative Protestant bodies. Accredited regionally within the last two years, the college enrolled 531 students in the fall of 1961.

Purposes of College D

1. To lead students to a fuller knowledge and a deeper appreciation of the Bible as the inspired Word of God (in accordance with the college motto—*Thy Word Is Truth*) and to a personal commitment to its teachings.

2. To guide students into a genuine Christian experience, to stimulate the development of Christian character, to nurture life in the Holy Spirit, and to foster the achievement of a well-integrated Christian personality.

3. To lead students to an appreciation of New Testament faith and practice as historically interpreted by the Church, to inspire a wholehearted acceptance of its principles, and to help make adjustments to a way of Christian living that gives expression to the sanctions of the Church as set forth in the Articles of Faith.

4. To help students acquire methods of correct thinking and effective communication; habits that promote physical competence; and understandings that lead to proper social adjustments.

5. To lead students to an appreciation of the cultural and practical values of the arts and sciences and to find Christian purpose in their use.

6. To help students discover vocational aptitudes, to help in the development of vocational skills, and to inspire Christian achievement in the performance of vocational duties.

7. To help students achieve the Christian ideal in marriage and home relationships and in various pursuits of life, especially rural life.

8. To qualify students to serve in various fields of Christian activity in the local congregation, in world-wide missions, and in various forms of evangelism for a universal witness of Jesus Christ.

Institution E.   Institution *E* is a four-year Protestant liberal arts college in the deep South, long regionally accredited and having a chapter of Phi Beta Kappa. It enrolled approximately 1,100 students in the fall of 1961. The current statement of purpose was developed by the faculty and approved by the board of trustees in 1960.

Purposes of College E

College *E* is a liberal arts college of the Church. As a collegiate institution rather than a university, it is concerned primarily with undergraduate education. The college's purposes are shaped, at all times, by its recognition of itself as a college dedicated to the production of a certain kind of graduate.

An Image of its Product

College *E* expects its graduates to be men and women of integrity who think, feel, and act individually. It does not pretend that a single projected image of graduates will precisely fit any two graduates, but it affirms its belief in perpetuating a common heritage on which authentic individualism may best be built. Such a common heritage, then, with its truly liberating capacity, constitutes the distinctive mark of the liberal education at College *E*. The college envisions its graduate as a person who is well-informed, discriminating, articulate, historically-rooted, and genuinely human.

The *well-informed* graduate, although particularly competent in a selected area, is widely read in other major fields of human interest. His is a knowledge which has truly "set him free"—to question and to accept ideas and to see ideas in new relationships and in broader contexts.

The *discriminating* graduate is at once capable of critical and appreciative thinking. He limits himself to no one mode of thought but moves freely in the realms of the scientific, the esthetic, the ethical, and religious. He carries his critical discrimination into his moral judgments; and out of his wide human sympathies, he seeks a personal life of ordered values in an ordered society.

The *articulate* graduate is, of necessity, the graduate who speaks and writes his native language competently; he is also the graduate whose exposure to ideas has been broad enough that he is conversant with the theoretical and the practical. His responses are limited neither by geographical nor by specialization barriers. He is unhampered by provincialism.

The *historically-rooted* graduate is he who responds to the new demands of a new day but retains always his appreciation of the past and its lessons. His respect for his heritage is neither sentimental nor chauvinistic. His religious aspirations and convictions stem from his active participation in his religious heritage.

The *genuinely human* graduate is, of course, the epitome of the virtues here listed. He is useful, productive, civic-minded, actively engaged in the promotion of human well-being; he is physically active, emotionally mature, intellectually alert, and spiritually well-poised; in short, he is the whole man.

Complementary Ideals and Objectives

The college's basic objective, that of producing the genuinely human graduate, is further reflected in the following set of ideals:

A. *Christian Commitment and [church] Identification.*
  1. As a liberal arts college of Christian heritage and outlook, College *E* is committed to:
     a. maintaining on its campus an atmosphere conducive to the developing and maturing of Christian faith and character; and
     b. providing, as an integral part of its liberal arts curriculum, courses in which the Biblical and historical foundations of Christianity are explored and courses in which the role and relevance of Christian faith in contemporary life are studied.
  2. As a church-sponsored institution the college acknowledges basic obligations to the [church]. The college recognizes its responsibility to:
     a. identify itself with the [church] in sponsorship of religious programs, and to
     b. provide within its liberal arts curriculum a program of pre-theological studies for ministerial students of the [church].

Mindful, however, of the broad non-sectarian spirit of the [church] at its best, the college does not impose denominational restrictions on faculty, staff, or student body; instead, it invites persons of other denominations and faiths to share in the life and work of the college in an atmosphere not merely of tolerance but of active good will. Furthermore, the college recognizes its obligation to students of other denominations and faiths and seeks to provide them with ample opportunity to cultivate their religious life in their own manner and conviction.

Cognizant of these obligations, the college affirms its conviction that its best service to the church is that of performing well its educational function as a liberal arts college.

B. *Intellectual Integrity, Academic Freedom, and Moral Responsibility.*

The college presupposes intellectual integrity on the part of its faculty and recognizes as a prime objective the cultivation of its students' intellectual integrity. Academic freedom, undergirded by a sense of moral responsibility, is both a condition of, and an expression of, intellectual integrity. Accordingly, the college seeks not to promote among its faculty uniformity of opinion but a willingness to test ideas by appeal to the methods of science, historical research, and other techniques of empirical inquiry in matters of fact; in areas calling for ethical, esthetic, and religious sensitivity, it attempts to cultivate and respect historically informed standards of discrimination. In all cases, the college seeks to confront ideas with ideas, not in a trial of strength but in free inquiry and mutual respect.

Institution F. Institution *F* is an institution for men in the far West, conducted by the Jesuits. Regionally accredited since 1952, the college enrolled in the fall of 1961 something over 1,000 students. The "purpose and scope" of the college appear in the following published statement:

The basic goal of College *F* is leadership in Christian humanistic studies. The mission of the college, therefore, is to provide this type of educational opportunity for young men who have the capacity and desire to benefit a modern society which needs leaders trained in this intellectual and moral tradition.

They may be described as "gifted generalists," men whose background and training enable them to deal with the highly specialized problems of our society. Their mental scope and perspective permits them to range outside their specialties to operate on a more encompassing level. They have specialized but are not trapped within the boundaries of their special field.

To this goal of broad intellectual accomplishment College *F* adds moral maturity so that *F* graduates can exemplify "the true Christian product of Christian education, the supernatural man who thinks, judges and acts, constantly and consistently in accordance with right reason, illuminated by the supernatural light of the example and teachings of Christ." (Pope Pius XI, Encyclical on The Christian Education of Youth.)

Perhaps the best description of the goal of the college is the definition of the graduate College *F* endeavors to produce: Such a man would be one who possesses a reflective mind which seeks premises as well as structure of the argument; who entertains opposing theses with calm dispassion and is fully aware that forms of procedure do not necessarily determine goals and certainly are not to be confused with them; who is eager to be well informed; who respects the knowledge of the past because he is aware of the great lessons of history; who looks forward as well as backward and is deeply concerned with decision and action. Additionally, the college strives to give the student an awareness that books are the basic tools of the educated man and to stimulate a consequent love of reading, both for pleasure and information, which will remain.

The faculty at College *F* is composed of Jesuit priests and dedicated laymen in about equal numbers. All share a deep respect for devout scholarship which is the basis of good teaching which, in turn, contributes inestimably to the formation of good character.

The previous statements of purpose appear to the author fairly representative of the variation to be found among colleges related to churches. The cited statements are more articulate than some; they are no more carefully wrought than many others.

Are stated objectives useful? The usefulness of stated objectives has long been under question. Many large, complex institutions do not state objectives, even in their individual units, because they assume that the functions of a university are simply to advance knowledge, transmit and criticize the heritage, and prepare for the professions.

Nevertheless, the regional agencies, led by the North Central Association in the nineteen thirties, had logic on their side in ruling that an educational institution ought to be judged mainly in terms of its own stated goals. The effort to define purposes has generally been a wholesome influence in higher education.

The difficulty is that a published statement has in itself no necessary power of virtue. The effectiveness of such declarations depends upon who creates them; how realistic they are in terms of resources, clientele, and educational appropriateness; how "visible" they are; and what efforts are being made to appraise educational results in terms of the purposes.

The previous illustrations of such statements indicate that the nature of stated purposes depends upon the academic sophistication of the institution and upon its basic religious orientation. A long-established, financially strong institution related to a liberal religious body will thus adopt objectives different in tone and emphasis from another of equal strength related to a more conservative group. In general, the more dependent the college is upon church support, the more emphasis upon religious goals there is likely to be in statements of purpose.

In the case of Roman Catholic colleges, there is unanimity as to philosophy, theology, and method (with emphasis upon training of the will) which is not possible for colleges related to the Protestant tradition.

The preceding statements of purpose, as well as most of the others represented in the group of colleges under study, have the following points in common:

Basic emphasis is placed upon the liberal arts, implemented by various distributive requirements to assure some familiarity with the major fields of knowledge and depth in at least one area. Although many of these institutions actually appear to specialize in teacher training or in business administration, they generally require substantial work in fields not related to the major.

There is almost universal agreement that the purposes of a church-related college require the cultivation of "mind and spirit" —a phrase often found in statements of purpose—with increasing emphasis on the primary intellectual dimension. There is still a reiteration that the educational experience must have an influence upon character but, far more than was shown in the Patton studies, there is insistence upon the need for rigorous intellectual standards. Whether or not this objective is being achieved is another problem.

By "spirit" most institutions which use the term appear to suggest that scholarship at its best always involves more than intellect alone, that full scholarship must help the student to become not only critical but *self-critical and self-judging*—capable of being at once both subject and object of criticism. Hence, there is increased effort to help the student to take sides on value questions, to commit himself on fundamental issues. Education at its best, in this context, involves dialogue, never mere transmission. The colleges would differ considerably regarding the interpretation of the common phrase "mind and spirit"; yet what has been suggested here is usually implied.[6]

A major aim of almost all the institutions under study is to develop familiarity with, understanding of, and commitment to the Judaeo-Christian tradition. The aim is implemented in many ways: by direct study of religion, theology, and/or the Bible; by the presence on campus of staff members who serve as teachers of religion, directors of religious life, and chaplains; by the presence of visitors especially able to make vivid the demands of the Christian faith; by opportunities for worship and work in religious service organizations; by appointment of faculty members who will strive to seek the religious implications in their respective disciplines.

The emphasis at this point will vary from the rigidly conservative religious institution, in which a pledge of theological belief may be exacted from faculty and staff (Institution *C*), to a more subtle and more liberal view of the relationship of the educational process to

---

6 For a useful interpretation of this argument from the point of view of the liberal Protestant, see Emerson W. Shideler, "A Protestant Doctrine of Education," *The Christian Century* (September 27, 1961).

religious commitment. This latter position is becoming prevalent and is expressed in the following definition of the Christian college by one articulate church-college president: "The college is principally a setting which the church makes possible in order that the processes of scholarship, of learning, of inquiry can confront and be confronted by the demands of Christian faith or the ultimate aspirations of Christians.[7]

The Roman Catholic does not, to be sure, find this view acceptable since he holds that the function of the Catholic college is to inculcate accepted Catholic doctrine in all Catholic students. Roman Catholic colleges do not, however, require non-Catholics to take courses in theology or to attend the Mass.

A major purpose of the church-related college, reiterated again and again in published statements, is the development of a community spirit in which intellectual endeavor and high moral purpose are dominant drives. Many people assume, however, that since the college is small and church-related, it is therefore a dynamic community. The faculties and trustees of many of these institutions are re-examining their opportunities and are using the vitality of their tradition to create a true community of scholars. There is also a growing awareness on the part of church colleges that the single most influential force on the student is the total campus atmosphere and that no naïve view of an externally imposed "spirit" is likely to be acceptable or effective.

The more liberal of these institutions hold that the fundamental requirements of a true community on a college campus are the following:

1. A sense of mutual purpose which, though it may not be unanimously acceptable, is nevertheless understood to set the orientation of the institution. This purpose must link excellence in intellectual demand with a concern for moral commitment.

2. A greater sharing in the establishment of college policy. In a true community no single group is subject to the sheer command of another group, and therefore new methods must be found to bring board of control, administration, faculty, and students into fruitful conversation.

---

[7] Orville W. Wake, "The Emerging Image of the Church College," *Encounter*, Vol. 22, No. 4, n.d.

3. A continuing and vital communication that must be maintained among all sectors of the campus.

Another common purpose of the church-related college is to identify, encourage, and inspire those who are or can be interested in church vocations. This is a direct and obvious service to the church. A study of enrollment in twelve Methodist theological seminaries in 1960–61 revealed that over 63 per cent of their students came from church-related institutions, 12 per cent from independent institutions, 23 per cent from public institutions, and approximately 2 per cent from foreign universities. Theological schools of other denominations report even larger percentages from church-related colleges.

A Few Persistent Questions

Annoying questions are raised by the foregoing summaries. For one thing, much of what has been stated as purpose requires careful rationalization and evaluation. Of all institutions of higher education, this group of colleges ought to be most sparing in its criticism of other institutions, most cautious in its claims, and most eager to learn the truth about its results. It appears to the author, however, that the church-related college is often most strident and shrill in its criticism of others, and most defensive in dealing with its own supposed virtues. On this point, too, institutions vary widely.

There is a tendency among the less sophisticated church-related colleges to assume that an objective is achieved because it has been publicly stated. Among this group of institutions there is far too little skepticism regarding actual results and not enough thoughtful effort at appraisal. Many church-related colleges are not as devoted to the liberal arts as their stated purposes suggest. There is more vocational training in these institutions than there was even three decades ago. Many are primarily teacher-training colleges. Nevertheless, there is still a strong tendency to insist that all students gain experience in the major fields of knowledge. Fully one-third of the more than 200 respondents to the questionnaire used in this study have recently restudied their curriculums in the light of basic purpose, and many of the revisions give high promise of stronger work in the liberal arts. Some institutions have radically cut their vocational offerings.

Every church college needs to ask itself again and again whether it is in fact dedicated to intellectual growth. There is a continuing suspicion that in many of these institutions intellectual rigor and excitement are subordinated to religious indoctrination, often because of sheer incapacity. A church-college campus ought, however, to be a place where ideas of every sort struggle for fair hearing, or, as Institution E stated in its purposes: "The college seeks to confront ideas with ideas, not in a trial of strength but in free inquiry and mutual respect."

Unless there is honest intellectual confrontation between faculty and student there is little hope that "education for decision" or "cultivation of the spirit" will be anything more than phrases; yet "mind and spirit" are indeed crucially related.

There is always danger in education of accepting the part for the whole. Thus church-related colleges are often taxed with using Biblical study and required chapel as the single characteristic of their uniqueness. Serious Bible study represents a major opportunity but cannot be the whole opportunity. A good deal of evidence suggests that courses in religion and Bible are increasingly taught by teachers at least as well-qualified as those in other disciplines. This is a great gain.

No purpose is more difficult to achieve than the development of a community ethos in which intellectual adventure is possible in an atmosphere of moral concern and commitment. Studies which have attempted to measure the changing value structures of college students show no evidence that church-related colleges are any more effective generally on this point than other types of institution. The well-known summary by Philip E. Jacob in *Changing Values in College* gives no comfort at all to church colleges.

If, therefore, there is any validity in the concept that the "community" created in a church-related college has in it any special potency, more sophisticated attention must be given to how such a community is produced and how its results may be tested. Much more thought must also be paid to such problems as faculty-administration and faculty-student relationships.

Professional education is still in the throes of general self-examination. In its preprofessional training the church-related college must give careful attention to recent studies of the problem. Further, if the church-related college is to be a chief source of supply for ministerial candidates and for other church vocations, then the most vigorous thought must be applied to the early needs of these preprofessional candidates. There is increasing concern about the problem among the colleges of this group. The concern must be backed up by severe study of what the responsibility entails.

CHAPTER V

Courses and Those Who Teach Them

An educational program can be evaluated intelligently only in terms of the stated objectives of the institution. Conversely, objectives are to be appraised in terms of what takes place on the campus. The true objectives of the institution are the practices of the institution. There is great variation in educational program among the institutions here under study, but numerous common factors emerge.

General Education

As a group, these institutions attempt to achieve their objectives in general education by the required courses demanded of all or of major segments of the total enrollment. In the senior colleges under study, the range of required courses varies from about 30 per cent to 60 per cent, with only a few exceptions.

A few illustrative cases follow, selected to show the variations among the institutions. Each refers to a regionally accredited college, using enrollment figures for the fall of 1961.

COURSES REQUIRED OF VIRTUALLY ALL STUDENTS
(Physical education omitted)

INSTITUTION A
(Enrollment 610—Southern—Protestant)

Course	Semester Hours
English	6
Religion	3
Psychology	3
* Humanities	6
* Natural Science	6
* Social Science	6
	30

* Integrated general courses.

INSTITUTION B
(Enrollment 650—Midwest—Protestant)

Course	Semester Hours
English	6
Religion and philosophy	6
Man and the physical world	6
Man and the theological world	3
Hygiene	3
Man and the social world	3
History of western civilization	3
Man and literature	6
Man and the fine arts	4
	40

INSTITUTION C
(Enrollment 647—Southeast—Women—Protestant)

Course	Quarter Hours
English	9
Bible	9
Foreign language	9–18
Literature	9
Science and mathematics	21
History or classics or philosophy	9
	66–75

INSTITUTION D
(Enrollment 559—Northwest—Women—Catholic)

Course	Semester Hours
* Theology	12
Philosophy	12
World literature	12
Foreign language	12–16
Science	8
History	6
Political science	3
	65–69

* Not required of non-Catholics.

INSTITUTION E
(Enrollment 920—Southwest—Protestant)

Course	Semester Hours
Integrated religion, philosophy, history	12
English	6
Foreign language	12.
Science	12
Senior capstone (Christianity and contemporary problems)	3
	45

INSTITUTION F
(Enrollment 2070—Far West—Protestant)

Course	Semester Hours
English	6
Development of civilization	8
Study of man and mankind	3
Family life	2
American history and culture	6
Science	8–12
Functions of democracy	3
Religion or philosophy	3
Foreign language	0–8
	39–51

INSTITUTION G
(Enrollment 1851—Midwest—Interdenominational)

Course	Semester Hours
Bible	16
English	3
Speech	2
Fine arts	2
Foreign language	12
Literature	6
Social science	6
Military science	4
	51

INSTITUTION H
(Enrollment 1750—New England—Men—Catholic)

Course	Semester Hours
English	12
Mathematics	6
* Theology	16
Philosophy	28
Foreign language	12
History	12
* Not required of non-Catholics.	86

The range of required courses in this sampling is from one-fourth of the total needed for graduation (Institution A) to nearly three-fourths (Institution H). In each case, some of the general requirements will apply toward majors or minors, and in all the instances cited proficiency tests or demonstrated competence may shorten the total.

Several generalizations are applicable. Roman Catholic colleges almost invariably demand more specific courses than their non-Catholic counterparts. Roman Catholic institutions also demand far more religion and philosophy, though theology is not required of non-Catholic students. Two of the eight institutions [1] require no foreign language, either for admission or for graduation, and one of the others among the illustrations will accept two years of high school foreign language as meeting the requirement.

Nearly one of every four colleges in the special sampling includes within its required program at least one integrated general course, and many more of the colleges are talking about the development of such programs. Among characteristic revisions of traditional courses are such as these:

1. "Freshman English" revised to "Introduction to the Liberal Arts." (A course to orient and to improve writing, speaking skills.)
2. English surveys (English, American, World Literature) revised to "Masterpieces of World Literature." (Using mainly whole books, chiefly paperbacks, and usually including Oriental literature.)
3. Long humanities sequences (two, three, and four years).
4. Introductions to Western Civilization (emphasizing the Hebraic-Christian heritage and its relationship to other ancient cultures).

---

[1] One of these is now discussing the addition of a language requirement.

The list could be made much longer and would include senior integrative courses created to serve as capstones for the educational programs. Many of these colleges are experimenting with independent study, and some, such as The College of Wooster (Ohio), are pioneers in the field.

There are clauses in many of the degree programs to enable students in special areas—notably music, home economics, physical education, education, and business—to escape some of the basic requirements listed above. There are degrees—for example, the bachelor of science in education—which may omit the foreign language otherwise required. In many music and business education programs, foreign language is omitted. Actually, there are opposing views evident as to the purpose and value of foreign language study, but many institutions have recently added relatively expensive language laboratories.

Majors tend to range between 24 and 36 semester hours—again except for music, home economics, and business administration. There is a growing tendency for mathematics and the sciences to require more than the 24 hours beyond the basic courses. Elementary education in many of the institutions is a special case and usually has very heavy requirements in methods. This is due as a rule, however, to having state requirements for certification.

Proliferation

The unhappy proliferation of courses so common to the nineteen forties and nineteen fifties seems to have run its course among the senior colleges under study. The chief reasons for the slowing down are harsh financial realities which now become compelling. The same problem of proliferation exists in the larger public institution, but in the small college of modest means its results can be catastrophic.

The initiating causes of the proliferation are very near the surface. For one thing, faculty members are always eager to teach their specialties. Many institutions in the past offered excessive numbers of courses in the hope, usually false, of attracting substantially more students. Others chose to try to compete with larger, more affluent institutions even at the point of variety of offerings. Nearly everyone forgot, or chose not to follow the common sense injunction of the philosopher Alfred North Whitehead: "Do not teach too many subjects; what you teach, teach well."

Earl McGrath in *Memo to a College Faculty* [2] has well-documented the current situation in fourteen colleges, twelve of which are church-related. His figures follow:

ENROLLMENTS 1958–59 AND CREDIT HOURS OF INSTRUCTION OFFERED IN THE ACADEIMC YEAR 1957–58 PLUS ADDITIONAL CREDIT HOURS OF DIFFERENT COURSES OFFERED DURING 1958–59 [3]

	1	2	3
	1958–59 Enrollments	Credit Hours Offered	Ratio of Column 2 to Column 1
	620	1117	1.80
	734	1114.5	1.52
	785	773.5	.99
	844	1242	1.47
	910	834	.92
	938	1387	1.48
	1011	1147.5	1.14
	1015	1321	1.30
	1025	1174.5	1.15
	1145	914.5	.80
	1155	1048	.91
	1164	1126	.97
	1228	1069.5	.87
	1591	1124	.71
Range	620–1591	773.5–1387	.71–1.80
Median	1013	1120.5	1.07

In an even more revealing chart, McGrath has shown the range in departmental offerings for the same fourteen institutions:

---

[2] Earl J. McGrath, *Memo to a College Faculty* (New York: Teachers College, Columbia University, 1961).

[3] Programs in music and art including a large number of performance and studio courses were omitted from this and other tables because they distort the average so decidedly toward the low end of the scale. None of the tables incorporates figures on ROTC or AFROTC programs. Separate calculations revealed that the ranks of the institutions in Column 1 would have remained substantially the same if enrollments for both years had been used. In Column 2, credits for courses offered in 1958–59 were added to the total only if they had not been offered in 1957–58.

RANGES OF CREDIT HOURS OFFERED IN MAJOR SUBJECTS—
14 SELECTED COLLEGES

	Credit Hours		Difference Between Minimum and Maximum
Subject	Minimum	Maximum	
Biology	38	98	60
Chemistry	37.5	83.5	46
Classical Languages	42	53	11
Economics	39	84	45
Economics and Business Administration	51	108	57
Business Administration	33	73	40
Education	38	82	44
English	54	146	92
French	27	64	37
Geology	37.5	58	20.5
German	22	52	30
History	42	81	39
Home Economics	41	54	13
Mathematics	38	94	56
Philosophy	30	57	27
Philosophy and Religion	51	91	40
Physics	37.5	73	35.5
Political Science (Government)	27	81	54
Psychology	21	71	50
Religion (Bible)	25	48	23
Sociology	24	64	40
Sociology and Anthropology	36	53	17
Spanish	24	63	39

The critical facts in the McGrath report which apply fully to the colleges here under study are these:

1. The largest institutions in some instances offered fewer courses than the smaller ones. The smallest institution in the sampling, and the one with the highest ratio, offered more credit hours than another institution two and one-half times the size of the first.

2. The ratio of credit hours offered to enrollment ranged from 0.7 to 1.80.

Close examination of statistics from other selected church-related colleges affirms the same general findings. Following are a few cases chosen at random to illustrate the small-class problem which usually emerges from a proliferated curriculum:

Institution A. Unaccredited, Midwestern, enrolling 527 students, offering 21 majors (excluding music and physical education) and 610 credit hours. Ratio of enrollment to credit hours—1:1.15.

Class Size at Institution A

Classes enrolling over 10	49 per cent
Classes from 5–10	19 per cent
Classes enrolling fewer than 5	32 per cent

The excessive instructional costs of such a program are self-evident, and one may ask as well about the intellectual challenge in so many classes with fewer than five students.

Institution B. Southern, accredited, enrolling 610 students, offering 19 majors and 649 credit hours (excluding music and physical education). Ratio of enrollment to credit hours—1:1.06.

Class Size at Institution B

Classes enrolling from 25–75	28 per cent
Classes enrolling 11–24	35 per cent
Classes enrolling 5–10	23 per cent
Classes enrolling 1–4	14 per cent

This is a more favorable picture than that of Institution *A*, financially at least; yet even here 37 per cent of all classes had fewer than 11 students.

Institution C. Northeast, accredited, enrolling 1200 students, offering 19 majors and 1061 credit hours (excluding music and physical education). Ratio of enrollment to credit hours—1:0.88.

Class Size at Institution C

Classes enrolling 25 and over	27 per cent
Classes enrolling 11 to 25	51 per cent
Classes enrolling 5 to 10	14 per cent
Classes enrolling fewer than 5	8 per cent

These samples are characteristic of the group under study. The centrifugal forces on a campus tend to extend the edges of the curriculum further and further from the core. One of these forces is departmental imperialism, which works to increase the size of the department and, inevitably, the offerings as well. Fortunately, nearly one of every five of the 200 questionnaires returned for this study indicated that curriculums, including numbers of majors, were being cut, with probable benefit to the entire program.

Two illustrations of what is being done suggest attempts to parallel offerings with resources. One college in the Southwest in five years clipped its total course offerings from 738 to 412 and halved the number of different degrees offered. As courses were cut, teachers taught fewer subjects at one time; independent study was added; and, perhaps most immediately important, salaries were advanced markedly. Actually, the educational program was strengthened in the process. Another college in the Midwest dropped more than 200 courses in one year, developed several comprehensive general education sequences, eliminated entirely a number of vocational curriculums, and neared its goal of much higher salaries.

Studies now being conducted by some of this group lead in the same direction. There are, however, far more institutions with no such plans in mind, unconsciously choosing perhaps to continue a diffusion of their power. For these the days ahead are even more perilous than the present.

Department heads and deans of small colleges would do well to note the quotations cited by McGrath, particularly that of one department head in biology:

> My aim as head of the biology department has been to prevent teachers from spreading themselves too thin and trying to teach everything that could be included under a biology curriculum. It seems to me more reasonable to have each one teach an introductory course and two additional courses. . . . If you will look over our offerings, you will find that the active fields of biology are well represented, but that we do not offer many specialized or restricted areas except [in a few cases where the instructor is particularly well qualified].[4]

Offerings in Religion. More than 95 per cent of all the senior colleges in the sampling of 200 under study offer a major in religion, or a combination major in religion-philosophy. In the Catholic institutions, "theology" is the characteristic designation for courses in religion, although in some the bulletins list curriculums in both religion and theology.

---

[4] Earl J. McGrath, *Memo to a College Faculty* (New York: Teachers College, Columbia University, 1961), p. 21.

The same proliferation of courses is to be found in religion departments as in others. Catalogues have been examined in which there are as many as 100 hours of religion and religious education. In some of the cases examined, fully one-third of the courses listed in proliferated departments had not been taught in a three-year span —glowing examples of bulletin "window-dressing." In some institutions, professionalized work in religious education appears also to deny the avowed liberal arts emphasis of the college.

A few examples suggesting the scope of work in religion will illustrate the variety to be found:

> *Institution A.* Protestant, Northeast, 1200 students. *Religion:* 7 courses; 21 semester hours. (In addition 6 hours of independent study and projects in the field.)
>
> *Institution B.* Protestant, Southeast, 650 women. *Bible and religion:* 18 courses; 84 quarter hours.
>
> *Institution C.* Catholic, Northeast, 1800 men. *Theology:* 9 courses; 32 semester hours.
>
> *Institution D.* Protestant, Southwest, 600 students. *Religion:* 13 courses; 39 semester hours.
>
> *Institution E.* Protestant, South, 650 men. *Religion:* 6 courses; 18 semester hours. (Additional courses available in campus School of Theology.)

A good deal of thinking needs to be done by these colleges on the question of what constitutes an effective, though non-professional, major in religion.

The Professor and the College Program

All academic programs finally depend for their success on the faculty and students involved. It is impossible, and fortunately unnecessary, to say which of these factors—faculty or students—is more important. Data regarding faculty strength are both hard to come by and difficult to appraise. Here will be applied, however, a few of the more common measurable tests of quality, with full awareness of their extreme limitations.

Preparation. In order to appraise faculty preparation, the author examined in detail the percentage of faculty members holding doctorates in all institutions in seven states involved in this study: California, Illinois, Ohio, Michigan, Pennsylvania, Georgia, and Texas. Only accredited institutions were used, since it appears self-evident that a major problem of the unaccredited college is likely to be the adequacy of the faculty. No attempt was made to appraise the faculties of church-related junior colleges, although there is evidence that these are being generally upgraded.

PERCENTAGES OF DOCTORATES ON FACULTIES OF CHURCH-RELATED COLLEGES IN SELECTED STATES (1958–59)

State	Number of Institutions	Percentage		
		Highest	Median	Lowest
California	24	78	43	15
Georgia	11	71	32	20
Illinois	22	64	38	18
Michigan	14	62	36	20
Ohio	26	78	38	12
Pennsylvania	42	89	35	14
Texas	21	68	33	23
	160*			

* Incomplete data for 2 institutions.

There is tremendous variation in the percentage of doctorates in individual institutions among the 160 under consideration. If the percentage of doctorates on a faculty is a significant index of faculty strength, some of these institutions are very strong indeed while others are weak. When fewer than 20 per cent of a faculty of a senior college have achieved the doctorate, there is room for improvement.

When the breakdown is made by size of institution, the following median percentages develop:

MEDIAN PERCENTAGE OF DOCTORATES BY ENROLLMENT

Enrollment	Number of Institutions*	Median Percentage
To 300	13	34
301–600	42	41
601–1000	53	34
1001–2000	41	39
Over 2001	11	36

* Incomplete data for 2 institutions.

Faculty-student ratios. The relevance of faculty-student ratios to institutional excellence has long been in contention. Once it was almost automatically assumed that a low ratio of faculty to students meant quality in education. Today the relation is highly debatable. For the institutions in the seven states noted, the faculty-student ratios (using fall enrollments) were:

NUMBER OF STUDENTS PER FACULTY MEMBER—
CHURCH COLLEGES IN SEVEN SELECTED STATES

(Based on Full-Time Equivalent Students and Faculty)

Frequency	Students Per Faculty Member
22	1–10
49	11–14
57	15–18
12	19–20
22	Over 20
	Median 15

Several generalizations are possible from these figures. Nearly 15 per cent of the colleges in the seven-state sampling now have ratios of 1:20 or over. They are thus at or beyond the 1:20 ratio suggested as essential in the Ruml[5] proposals. Whether this is a sign of weakness or of careful planning, it is not possible to say with the data at hand. A 1:20 ratio is not in itself a proof of institutional weakness.

Salaries. The financial structures of colleges represent the major test of ability to perform sound educational work. The entire problem is treated in some detail in Chapter VII, but here attention is given to the most crucial of all financial data: the salaries of the teaching staff.

A comprehensive study of faculty salaries for the year 1961–1962 by the U.S. Office of Education[6] produced the following summary:

---

[5] Beardsley Ruml and Donald H. Morrison, *Memo to a College Trustee* (New York: McGraw-Hill Book Company, Inc., 1959).

[6] W. Robert Bokelman, Louis A. D'Amiko, and Ann Jane Holbrook, "Salaries and Basic Student Charges at Private Controlled Institutions of Higher Education," *Educational Record,* Vol. 44, No. 3 (July, 1963).

AVERAGE 1961–62 SALARIES OF FACULTY PERSONNEL (FOUR RANKS COMBINED) IN UNDERGRADUATE 4-YEAR INSTITUTIONS, BY TYPE OF CONTROL AND FOR 9-10 MONTH CONTRACTS

TYPE OF INSTITUTIONAL CONTROL	9–10 MONTH CONTRACTS		
	—— Number ——		Average
	Inst.	Indiv.	Salary
Public and private combined	794	79,873	$7,665
Total public	274	49,424	7,918
Total private	520	30,449	7,256
Private Institution Affiliation			
Independent	161	15,005	$8,104
Baptist	27	1,457	6,329
Lutheran	23	1,502	6,552
Methodist	60	3,265	6,382
Presbyterian	44	1,784	6,398
Catholic	142	4,821	6,473
All other	63	2,615	6,433

AVERAGE 1961–62 SALARIES OF FACULTY PERSONNEL IN 2-YEAR INSTITUTIONS BY TYPE OF CONTROL AND FOR 9–10 MONTH CONTRACT

TYPE OF INSTITUTIONAL CONTROL	9–10 MONTH CONTRACTS		
	—— Number ——		Average
	Inst.	Indiv.	Salary
Public and private combined	305	10,469	$6,836
Total public	208	8,558	7,207
Total private	97	1,911	5,175
Private 2-year Institution Affiliation			
Independent	35	895	$5,628
Baptist	18	325	4,601
Lutheran	6	65	5,064
Methodist	14	252	4,751
Presbyterian	7	105	4,736
Catholic	9	50	4,301
All other	8	219	5,103

These figures indicate that faculty salaries in church-related colleges as a group tend to average from $1,500 to $1,700 per year lower than in independent institutions and almost the same amount below public institutions. In the two-year colleges the differential between church-related and independent ones is about $1,000; but between church-related and public ones it is more nearly $2,500. In the junior colleges, the figures for public institutions are much influenced by the relatively high salaries in California.

Average faculty salary figures do not suggest the wide variations among church-related colleges. To study these differences more closely, the author selected at random the reports of 64 senior colleges of the group under study.[7] Of the 64 reports, 12 were unwilling to report faculty salaries—leaving 52 as the sample group, just under 10 per cent of the total four-year colleges under study and representing 22 states. It might, of course, be inferred that colleges not willing to divulge salaries have lowest salary scales. Only the salaries of professors (those with the highest academic rank) are represented in the following chart:

AVERAGE SALARIES 1960–61—PROFESSORS ONLY
(Nine-Month Contracts, Random Sample—52 Colleges[7]—22 States)

High	$9,880
Median	7,535
Low	5,192

One must remember that these are institutional averages and that some salaries were above the "high" given here and others below the "low."

Among 40 of the 52 reports, the only ones usable on the point, the median salary increase for professors between 1955 and 1960 was 40 per cent, with some as high as 75 per cent. Since 1950, however, the median salary increase for professors has been well over 100 per cent. There is obviously a strong movement in the right direction, but relatively the position is still not favorable.

Every college which filled out the detailed questionnaire noted that the major problem of the future was adequate faculty staffing. With no exception salaries are held to be among the chief deterrent to these colleges in the competitive situation of the 1960's. Special fears were registered by the respondents regarding staffing in the sciences, mathematics, psychology, and sociology.

Retirement and other benefits. There are almost no church-related senior colleges which have not developed some type of retirement plan, though nearly 20 per cent cooperate in only the

---

[7] These are all regionally accredited institutions.

federal social security program. About 30 per cent of the two-year colleges have more than the federal minimum. Since a large proportion of the faculties of Roman Catholic institutions are members of a religious community, the retirement problem for these institutions appears unique. Many lay teachers, however, are also employed in Catholic colleges and retirement programs must be provided for them. Illustrations of the various types of retirement programs in effect in 1961 follow:

Institution A is Midwestern, Protestant, and in 1961 enrolled 1,100 students. The college employs the Teachers Insurance Annuity Association plan, contributing 8 per cent from college funds and receiving 2 per cent from salary checks—or 10 per cent in all. Up to 50 per cent of the Teachers Insurance Annuity Association funds may be used in the College Retirement Equities Fund plan.

Institution B is Northeastern, Roman Catholic, and in 1961 enrolled 848 full-time men. The college provides an insurance-annuity to which the institution contributes 5 per cent of salary and the individual a like amount. It is compulsory after three years of service.

Institution C is Southeastern, Protestant, and in the fall of 1961 enrolled 1,374 full-time students. The retirement plan applies only to faculty members on tenure, with the college contributing 10 per cent to the Teachers Insurance Annuity Association. Half of the premium may be used to purchase a variable annuity from the College Retirement Equities Fund.

Institution D is deep South, Protestant, and in the fall of 1961 enrolled 970 full-time students. Pretenure faculty members and those on tenure less than five years may participate in the retirement program with the college paying 7½ per cent to the Teachers Insurance Annuity Association program and the individual 7½ per cent. For those on tenure five years or longer, the college itself pays 15 per cent of salary to the Teachers Insurance Annuity Association program.

Institution E is a men's college in the Southwest, Roman Catholic, and in the fall of 1961 enrolled 1,505 students. The college matches the individual's payment of 5 per cent for the purchase of a trust fund which becomes the individual's at age sixty-five.

The largest contribution to a retirement program on the part of a senior college in the group studied is 15 per cent. The median is

5 to 6 per cent, and the low is only social security benefits. The junior colleges are just beginning to plan such programs.

Housing. A major problem among these institutions, notably the ones in rural areas, involves housing of faculty members, new ones in particular. Most colleges in the sampling own a few houses and apartments which may be rented by new faculty members at modest rates. Many colleges have been unable to do anything about the housing problem except to help faculty in the search for houses. There are, however, a surprising number—nearly 10 per cent of the group—which have developed plans to help faculty members purchase their own homes. A few of these plans are noted here, though they are far from typical of the entire group.

Institution A in the rural South, guarantees housing for every faculty member and offers low interest loans for those wishing to build their own homes.

Institution B, in the rural Midwest, reports the following plan:

> The apartments which were completed during the last year consist of nine two-bedroom units, which are rented to new staff members on a three-year rotating basis. In other words, no staff member may live in the units more than three years, and in this manner they are available for new staff members as they are employed. We have three other small apartments which consist of 21 units. In addition, we have 30 individual residences which we rent to our staff. Considering the four apartments and the 30 individual residences we have a total of 60 rental units. About eight years ago, we plotted 19 acres of real estate around our observatory into 53 residential lots. We sell the lots to our staff members and, if necessary, assist in the financing of their houses. About one half of this area has been developed and 29 homes have been built. In all probability the remaining lots will be built upon during the next five years.

Institution C in the urban south, reports as follows:

> A staff member on tenure has the privilege of building a home on [X] Road on a lot furnished by the college. The college will lend up to 90 per cent of the cost of construction at 4 per cent annual interest, payable over a maximum of twenty-five years, and the house is tax exempt. If the owner leaves the college, the house must be sold to another faculty member within two years or the college will buy it at the fair market value. Spouses of deceased staff members may continue residence on Faculty Row as long as they make necessary payments on the house and do not remarry.

These are, of course unusually favorable programs from the point of view of faculty retention. Though there are other plans like them, these are not as yet typical.

Eighty per cent of the four-year colleges, and a majority of the two-year institutions, offer health insurance programs like Blue Cross and Blue Shield; but barely 40 per cent of the senior colleges and only a few of the junior colleges have any kind of major medical insurance programs for the faculty. Major medical insurance programs are designed to provide significant financial aid in cases of prolonged or catastrophic illness. The data suggest, though not conclusively, that well over half of the four-year colleges share with the faculty members the cost of health insurance programs, but only a small number give major medical assistance.

Teaching loads.   It was not possible to secure precise data on teaching loads in the colleges under study. The following generalizations, however, are supported by the data at hand:

Expectedly, lower teaching assignments are to be found among the larger, more affluent institutions. Colleges with enrollments under 750 tend to expect 12 to 15 hours of teaching per week, with the median of actual teaching hours per week near 14. Exceptions are music and home economics, where loads are often much higher.

Among at least one-fourth of the four-year church colleges, and especially in colleges enrolling over 1,500 students, teaching loads tend to be 12–13 hours, with two hours of laboratory instruction counting as one teaching hour.

Nearly 50 per cent of the senior colleges make a load adjustment, usually 3 hours, for department or division heads. It is increasingly common also for English teachers to have loads of 12 hours even when the normal assignment is 14–15.

In colleges under 750, the average number of different courses taught by a single instructor during a term tends to approach four in schools on the semester system and three in schools on the quarter system. In the larger institutions three separate courses are near the norm. Nevertheless, there are substantial numbers of cases in which as many as five different courses are taught at one time by a single instructor. The difficulty of keeping up-to-date in such circumstances is self-evident.

Many teachers with four and five separate courses may still carry a relatively low student credit-hour load, due to small enrollments in upper-division courses. This is again a result of the proliferation of advanced courses, particularly in institutions of small enrollments.

There is now a slight tendency, which appears to be growing among these institutions, to consider a three-course program for all students, which would tend to cut down the number of preparations per faculty member. Nearly 10 per cent of the senior colleges under study either report adoption of such plans or say they are considering them.

Perhaps the most serious educational problem in the smaller institution is the one-man department. In such cases, students get virtually all their major work from one man, with obvious handicaps for the student. The difficulty for the faculty member is even more devastating. When a faculty member is overloaded, especially in the number of discrete preparations, it is quite unlikely that he will have the energy or the will for creative scholarship, upon which his own development is so closely dependent. Again, however, there is wide varation among the institutions.[8]

Tenure. From a random sampling of somewhat more than 10 per cent of the total group of colleges under study, it is clear that tenure provisions fall mainly into the following categories:

1. Only about one-half the junior colleges have formulated any kind of tenure provisions, although the problem is under study in many more.

2. Roman Catholic colleges (junior and senior) are usually heavily staffed by members of the involved religious community, and tenure is not a major problem.

3. The larger Roman Catholic institutions and other senior colleges almost invariably have formal tenure programs—more than 90 per cent of those sampled. The median year of service for achieving tenure among these institutions is now the fourth. In all but a few cases faculty members transferring from other institutions must serve at least two years at the new institution before tenure is granted.

Retirement is mainly at age 65. Most institutions allow annual

---

[8] The problems outlined above are sharply delineated, for the small college in particular, by Lewis B. Mayhew, *The Smaller Liberal Arts College* (Washington, D.C.: The Center for Applied Research in Education, Inc., 1962).

contracts after age 65 until age 70, but only upon administrative-trustee invitation.

Academic freedom. The problem of academic freedom in a church-related college is approached in a variety of ways. About 75 per cent of all the senior colleges in the group studied have formally adopted as their own the official American Association of University Professors statement of 1940 on academic freedom. It is on the point of the "exceptions" to the freedom allowed in this statement that the major differences occur. Here again the colleges fall largely into three major groupings:

1. There is a small group in which there is *no* published pledge of academic freedom.

2. Some institutions require assent to a formal creed, either in writing or by verbal consent. If this is no restraint to freedom in any active sense, it at least assures prior agreement on certain points. There are a few institutions, notably in the South, which will neither place a man on tenure, nor make him a department head if he does not subscribe to the denomination's creed. The number in this category is also relatively small, but included are some influential institutions. These institutions "expect" no faculty member to teach concepts which contradict church principles or dogma.

3. The largest number by far require no assent to a creed, yet the administrative officers discuss with each candidate the total purposes of the institution to discover whether the candidate would feel "comfortable" in the situation. In many of these institutions teachers, particularly of religion and philosophy, tend to be members of the sponsoring denomination.

The following sampling of official statements on academic freedom is offered with the comment that on this point practice is often better than official formulations might suggest. Nevertheless church-related colleges have a problem here which demands close study.

College A, Protestant

Members of the faculty of College *A*, by virtue of their appointment, respect the religious, moral, and intellectual commitments involved in a sincere and voluntary profession of the evangelical Christian faith in Jesus Christ as Son of God and Saviour of the world and accept the obligations of membership in the Christian college that promotes the educational aims and purposes of the [sponsoring church].

Within the limits imposed by his voluntary acceptance of the conditions of his appointment as indicated above, and in accordance with the ideal of complete intellectual integrity, scholarly objectivity, and respect for the convictions of others, a member of the faculty is entitled to freedom of thought, research, and discussion in the treatment of his subject.

The college teacher is a citizen, a member of a learned profession, and an officer of an educational institution. When he speaks or writes as a citizen, or a private person, he should be cognizant of the fact that his special position in the community imposes special obligations. As a man of learning and an officer of the college, he should remember that, though he may properly disclaim being a spokesman for the college, yet the public may judge his profession and his institution by his utterances. Hence, he should be accurate at all times, should exercise appropriate objectivity and moderation, meet reasonable standards of propriety and good taste, and exhibit a respect for the convictions of others.

Cases involving abuse of academic freedom may be referred or may be appealed to a committee composed of three ranking members of the instructional staff elected by the faculty for this purpose, and two members of the board of regents. This committee shall make appropriate recommendations to the president of the college.

College B, Protestant

College *B* subscribes to the statement on academic freedom and tenure adopted jointly in 1940 by the Association of American Colleges and by the American Association of University Professors. The main points of this statement follow: The teacher is entitled to full freedom in research and in the publication of the results, subject to the adequate performance of his other academic duties. . . .

The teacher is entitled to freedom in the classroom in discussing his subject, but he should be careful not to introduce into his teaching controversial matter which has no relation to his subject. Limitations of academic freedom because of religious or other aims of the institution should be clearly stated in writing at the time of the appointment.

The teacher is entitled to his political rights as a citizen and "should be free from institutional censorship or discipline"; but he should remember that he is also a "member of a learned profession and an officer of an educational institution" and that "his special position in the community imposes special obligations . . . . Hence he should at all times be accurate, should exercise appropriate restraint, should show respect for the opinion of others, and should make every effort to indicate that he is not an institutional spokesman."

In accord with the above College *B* faculty members are expected to abide by the following statement adopted by the board of trustees and incorporated into each faculty member's contract:

"College *B* is a Christian institution, owned and controlled by the [sponsoring church]. Those employed by the [institution] to teach are expected to recognize their obligations by exhibiting an exemplary Christian life before the students and the public both inside and outside the college. According to the agreement concerning academic freedom and tenure approved by the board of trustees . . . teachers are expected to avoid the introduction into their teaching of controversial matters not related to their subjects. They should be especially careful to avoid making or approving any statements which run counter to the historic faith or the present work of [the church], and that so far as it is consistent with the professor's conscientious views and with his duties as a teacher, he shall advocate and advance the causes fostered by said denomination."

College C, Roman Catholic

Since freedom is necessary for the pursuit and dissemination of truth, faculty members may expect the utmost reasonable freedom in the exercise of their duties. But freedom is not license and reasonable freedom involves certain limitations. Hence, faculty members at Institution *C* will be expected not to uphold or teach religious doctrine opposed to Catholic faith, nor political doctrines subversive to the American form of government. No other limitations may be expected in any field, except those imposed by reason and truth.

College D, Protestant

College *D* shares in the generally accepted principle that colleges are designed to serve the common good and not to further the interest either of the individual teacher or the institution as ends in themselves. The common good depends on the free search for truth and its free exposition.

Academic freedom is essential to these purposes and it is fundamental for the protection of the rights of the teacher to teach and of the student to learn. It carries with it duties correlative with these rights.

Tenure is a means to certain ends; specifically: (1) freedom in teaching and in extra-mural activities; (2) a sufficient degree of economic security to make the profession attractive to men and women of ability. Upon freedom and economic security, and hence upon tenure, depends the success of an institution in fulfilling its obligations to its students and to society.

The instructor is entitled to freedom in the classroom in discussing all pertinent matters whether or not of a controversial nature.

College *D* is a church-related institution and in its principles, ideals, and aims seeks to be definitely Christian. It is expected that the members of the faculty will be Christian men and women thoroughly in sympathy with the moral and spiritual aims of the college.

College *D* recognizes that its teachers are citizens, members of a learned profession, and officers of an educational institution. When they speak or write as citizens, they shall be free from institutional censorship or discipline. It should be noted nevertheless that their special position in the community imposes special obligations. The public may judge their profession and their institution by their utterances; hence appropriate restraint and respect for the opinion of others are essential. Care should be exercised by an instructor to make clear that he is not a spokesman for the institution as a whole, especially where controversial issues are under consideration.

College E, Roman Catholic

The naturally sacred right of freedom of expression is, of course, recognized by College *E* as a requisite for effective and intelligent dissemination of ideas.

Nevertheless, there can be no such thing as unlimited freedom of expression in word and act. Besides the basic limitations upon freedom which arise out of the universally-accepted beliefs and mores of society, such as truthfulness, decency, moral integrity, and loyalty, there are those appropriate limitations which society expects in a Catholic college.

Consequently, all officers of instruction (also administrators) are expected to contribute to the objectives of the college by conforming to them, and by teaching nothing contrary to Catholic doctrine nor to American principles as these are embodied in the Declaration of Independence and the Constitution of the United States. All are expected to show a respectful and sympathetic attitude toward Catholic doctrine and American principles of government. Obviously any grave offense against these canons must be considered just cause for dismissal from College *E*.

The institution places no limitation upon freedom of teaching. It endeavors to employ Christian scholars, but without insistence upon any particular sectarian or theological position, and then it deliberately leaves these individuals free to teach truth as they understand it and know it.

In 1962 The American Association of University Professors submitted to the author a list of administrations censured between 1931 and 1962. The list numbered 51, of which 9 were among the group of institutions considered in this study, or somewhat less than 2 per cent of the total number of senior colleges.

Most church colleges, junior and senior, are making serious efforts to increase their ability to recruit and maintain faculties of power. That the task will be increasingly difficult goes without saying.

CHAPTER VI

Students and Student Services

The range of attention and intelligence given to student personnel services among church colleges is extraordinarily wide. In the smaller, less prosperous colleges there are likely to be a dean of men and a dean of women, usually not specially trained for their responsibilities, who are teachers at the same time. While there is logic in thinking that all deans in the smaller institutions (and perhaps in the larger ones too) should do some teaching so that they do not forget that the main business of the college is intellectual development, many of these deans teach nearly full loads. Obviously they cannot give professional attention or leadership to the student personnel programs of their institutions. At the other extreme there are church colleges in the 600–2,500 attendance range which have highly trained deans of students and carefully planned organizations and programs. In some of these institutions so strong a cleavage has developed between the faculty and the student personnel officers that the latter have no faculty status and do not teach classes.

Admissions. Admissions programs in many small church colleges are better termed "recruitment" programs. In spite of recent increases in student populations, numerous institutions still struggle to achieve a stable, economically-sized student body. Although these colleges have admissions standards, they are very low, and nearly any high school graduate can be admitted. There is no way of judging the number of such colleges, but it appears to be about 20 per cent of the senior colleges under study. The junior colleges are, in most instances, even more lenient, though there are some with strong admissions standards. To show the wide variation among the institutions, a few selected profiles of college admissions practices, as indicated by class standing and standardized tests, follow:

College A is Southern, coeducational, and unaccredited. It admits 95 per cent of those who apply and shows a tremendous range in the mental abilities among its student body. Among entering freshmen in 1958, the median percentile on the American Council on Education test was 22. At the same time, four students ranked above the ninetieth percentile. The great difficulty of working with a freshman class showing this range is of course obvious. The freshman class numbered 60.

College B shows a quite different pattern. Coeducational, Midwestern, and enrolling over 700 freshmen in 1961, the college admitted one of three of those who applied. Many who inquired about admission were, however, discouraged from filing papers. Ninety per cent of the class came from the top two-fifths of their high school classes, and 60 per cent of all students scored 500 or better on both the verbal and mathematical sections of the Scholastic Aptitude Tests of the College Entrance Examination Board. This is by no means among the most selective of senior colleges, but it is strong and most members of its student body are able to do good work.

College C is a college for women in the Southeast, admitting 196 girls in the fall of 1961. Only 18 of these came from outside the region. All but 42 girls scored 500 or above on the verbal Scholastic Aptitude Test and all but 59 scored above 500 on the mathematical test. Only 12 girls were not in the highest fifth of their high school graduating classes.

College D is a two-year college in the South, enrolling 145 freshmen in the fall of 1961. Slightly more than half of the class came from the bottom two-fifths of their high school classes; and while the college had room for 200 freshmen, it succeeded in recruiting only 145. Only eleven freshmen scored above 500 on the verbal Scholastic Aptitude Test, and only 13 scored above 500 on the mathematical section. Twenty-four scored below 299 on the verbal test and 16 below 299 on the mathematical. This is a more homogeneous, though much less talented, group than the more selective colleges can boast; but there is still the problem of providing for a few students who score over 500 on these tests.

General norms. The Center for the Study of Higher Education at Berkeley, California, reports the following mean test scores for students in various types of institutions. (A score of 100 for students entering higher education was recommended by The President's Commission on Higher Education.)

MEAN SCORES ON ACE PSYCHOLOGICAL TESTS BY TYPE OF CONTROL

Type	Mean Score
Private	113.2
Roman Catholic	111.7
Protestant	102.6
Public	100.9

In the Northeast, South, and West, according to this study, Roman Catholic institutions were highest in each case by a margin of one or two points. In the North Central area the Protestant schools were highest. More important, however, is this comment from the study: "The variation within any one of the categories of institutions was more striking than the difference among the classifications."[1] Precisely the same observation can be made about church-related colleges.

Many—perhaps over half of the church-related senior colleges— tend to become academically more restrictive. A substantial number are at full capacity and can afford to be more selective. Many others still find maximum tuition income necessary for survival and admit nearly everyone who applies.

One minor indication of the quality of students selecting church colleges today is to be found in the number of National Merit Scholars choosing these institutions. The following figures are from the Fourth Annual Report (1959–60) of The National Merit Scholarship Corporation. In that year 100 tax-supported institutions received 579 National Merit scholars,[2] or 5.79 per institution. In the same year, in 289 private institutions there were 2,357 scholars, or about 8.15 per institution. Of the 289 private colleges represented, 56 per cent, or 163, were church-related senior colleges enrolling 445 of the 2,357, or not quite 4 scholars per institution. Many of these colleges enrolled but a single scholar, while one small private college, not church-related, enrolled 55.

The senior colleges in the church-related group get up to 95 per cent of their students from within a range of fifty miles in the state

---

[1] T. R. McConnell and Paul Heist, "The Diverse College Student Population," in *The American College,* ed. Nevitt Sanford (New York: John Wiley & Sons, Inc., 1962), pp. 232–34.

[2] National Merit scholars receive substantial scholarships from a large number of business and other organizations. These students come mainly from the top 2 per cent of those taking the tests.

in which the college is located. Colleges in small rural towns are likely, however, to look to the nearest big city for students. Thus colleges in Iowa draw heavily upon Chicago for freshmen; one church-related institution in Iowa listed 281 students from Iowa and 343 from Illinois. This is a relatively common situation among similar colleges.

It is the rare church-related senior college which does not today have at least a small number of foreign students. In a sampling of fifty institutions with enrollments from 650 to 1,500 the number of foreign students ranged from five to eighteen. One church-related college in the Midwest, however, had a group of over forty Congolese, supported on full scholarships by churches in the state.

Seventy per cent of the senior colleges have more than 50 per cent of the student body living on campus, and some have as high as 95 per cent. In general, the schools with high percentages of students on campus are more or less rural, but there is an increasing number of urban church-related colleges steadily adding dormitory space. These urban colleges are trying to become more residential and less dependent upon local and commuting students.

Orientation.   The typical orientation program for freshmen in the church-related college has tended to be encompassed within a three- or four-day period. In many instances a convocation for freshmen and their parents is held on Sunday afternoon, at which time the purposes of the college are interpreted by the president, dean, or some faculty member. On Monday morning a battery of tests begins, mainly to determine which students, if any, should at once enter advanced courses in certain fields—usually English, mathematics, science, or foreign language. Sectioning by ability is generally used, especially in English, mathematics, and foreign language. It must be noted, however, that at least 20 per cent of the senior colleges in the sample group of 200 do not in fact use more than a psychological test and an English test; some use none at all. In too many instances the results of tests are not available until weeks later and have no usefulness whatever in planning the student's program. On the other hand an increasing number of institutions actually do section classes as a result of admission tests, and many of these place students at once into advanced courses.

After tests have been given, the students take campus tours; listen to talks by faculty members, administration, and officers of the student body; and meet their counselors. They are then ready, in the traditional orientation program, for registration.

There are encouraging exceptions to this type of orientation program. An increasing number of institutions are presenting the student with a list of three to five current books to read during the summer, to be discussed with faculty members during the orientation days.

The aim is meritorious and long overdue: to initiate the student at once into the intellectual life of the campus, and to stimulate from the beginning an interest in ideas, particularly those under general discussion. Such programs almost always meet with enthusiasm on the part of both student and faculty. The enthusiasm of faculty members is usually linked with surprise that freshmen are able to discuss ideas intelligently and that they are willing to make the effort to be ready for the discussion. In brief, orientation programs are under sharp revision, but the large majority of institutions appear still to believe that students must be herded from building to building, even on a small campus.

Counseling and guidance. On the smaller, less prosperous campuses, guidance is more or less casual and simple. The typical pattern is to assign each freshman to a faculty member as counselor, who is expected to help the student with his schedule and then keep in touch with him throughout the first two years. Often counselors have as many as thirty counselees, and too often the faculty member has little information about the student and little time to do any serious counseling with him. Normally the student who has declared his major will be assigned to the department in which he takes the major, and all juniors and seniors are assigned to the major professor.

There is no doubt that some good is done by counselors on this plan, but it can easily amount to very little. Particularly where there is an imaginative dean of students, some advances are being made, in group counseling, in developing a small group of competent faculty interested in more sophisticated work with selected students, and in student or semiprofessional counselors in dormitories. Where student-dormitory counselors are well-trained and carefully organized, advances can be made. On the whole, however, understaffed and overloaded student personnel offices cannot be expected to develop effective guidance programs. The lack of substantial guidance is doubtless one of the root causes of the heavy attrition in many small liberal arts colleges.

In a sizable group among the church-related colleges—both senior and junior—increasing attention and funds are being given to the guidance function. Some of these colleges have strong personnel offices, well-staffed and well-financed. In some there are professional counselors in each dormitory and student counselors on each floor of the dormitory. The counseling offices are able to refer students to psychiatrists with parents' permission, but the number of these institutions having even a part-time psychiatrist on the staff is negligible.

Among the weaker points in many guidance systems is a general lack of vocational counseling and placement services. Here again, however, there is a wide disparity among institutions, though almost none do as well as they would like to do.

It is becoming more and more common for the liberal arts colleges of the group to have annual or biennial career days, at which time leading exponents (often alumni) of major careers appear on campus for a day. This is a clear acknowledgment that to most students the life "in a job," which must accompany the life "of ideas," is an important concern.

A few colleges plan their convocation programs to bring to the campus a steady stream of visitors who speak about their work to the entire student body and then remain for at least a day to talk to any students who may wish further counsel. Only a small group of church-related colleges have worked out effective plans for such counsel, but the movement is growing.

Approximately one in ten of the colleges in the sample group has a placement office in the formal sense. Since teacher education is a major objective in many church-related colleges, some faculty member or committee is responsible for helping with teacher placement. There has been a shortage of teachers in most areas and placement has not been a severe problem. It is placement in other areas which has been neglected. Usually some administrative officer—one of the student deans or the dean of the college—will arrange for recruiting parties to meet appropriate students, but often this is done in haste and without careful planning. What is needed is a placement office directed by a full-time or near full-time person, with adequate secretarial help, to plan and carry forward a consistent program of vocational counseling and placement. The idea is spreading, but it is again slowed down by financial stringency.

Why should institutions which tend to be highly selective in the vocational training they offer be concerned about placement of graduates? The answer is that liberal arts graduates, often with no immediately salable skill, need help in learning how to approach employers and how to appear to best advantage. In the long run their education will make itself felt, but they need assistance in locating the kind of position in which their training can prove itself.

Health. The typical health program of the middle-sized church-related college is likely to show these general characteristics: The college will have a small building housing a clinic and infirmary, full-time nurse's quarters, and one ward for men and one for women with four to six beds in each. In addition there may be a two-bed room for the very temporary care of contagious diseases. The registered nurse will be on duty 24 hours a day, but with some relief either by a part-time assistant, by another full-time nurse, or by matrons in the dormitories. In some cases a section of the dormitory will be used for the clinic.

The clinic will be open formally during certain hours in the day, though the personnel deans may refer students to the clinic at any time. A physician or pair of physicians will be on campus perhaps five days a week, either the first thing in the morning or immediately following the lunch hour. Where there is a hospital nearby, the college will have worked out an arrangement to care for the more seriously ill there.

What has been described is the situation in the average institution in the group. There are institutions with much more elaborate facilities for taking care of health problems, but there are many which have little or nothing, with almost no service except perhaps a nurse dispensing simple drugs and referring problems to the local physicians. It is relatively rare, however, for rural colleges to be without a nurse and a small room in the dormitory serving as clinic. Junior colleges are frequently without even this minimum program.

Nearly all colleges require that the student's family physician fill out a simple health form before the student is admitted, but only about half of the senior colleges require further examinations on the campus by college physicians or by physicians employed for the purpose. Forms filled out by family doctors are not always useful.

In most institutions, a health fee helps to defray the expenses of whatever health services the college offers. Health insurance is more readily available, and is in some instances compulsory. It is increasingly common among the stronger institutions to have some provision for special diets for those who require it.

The problem of student health has not as yet been taken seriously by many church-related colleges. In many cases closer cooperation with a nearby hospital will likely produce better results than an attempt to develop a strong campus clinic.

Financial aid. The problems confronting church-related colleges in gaining necessary financial aid for their students are closely linked with the general financial structure of the institutions. Even in the institutions of highest prestige substantial scholarship aid is necessary if the colleges are to compete with other institutions in attracting students of top quality. In the weakest colleges, either scholarships or grants-in-aid are made to a large number of students in order to maintain an adequate enrollment. Originally, many church colleges were built to provide an education at low cost; it is now self-defeating to advertise a "cheap" educational program. Thus most of the colleges in the church-related sector offer the amount of scholarship necessary to get the kind of student body they want to have. At least 10 per cent of the senior colleges in this study now use the College Scholarship Service, however, before granting scholarships. (This service, sponsored by the College Entrance Examination Board, collects data on family resources of applicants and relates them to need, thus relieving the college of the responsibility of appraising actual student need.)

The major financial implications of scholarship programs arise out of the fact that a large proportion of the scholarships by the colleges are actually a charge against current income. Scholarship endowments and specially designated gifts as a rule do not begin to cover the amount of scholarship assistance needed. Indirectly, therefore, many of these scholarships may be considered charges against faculty salaries.

As tuition charges have risen, it has been necessary to raise grants so that the college involved does not limit itself to admitting only those who can pay. The principle is sound, but in the case of many institutions, scholarships and grants-in-aid (for those not qualified for scholarships) are merely methods of purchasing students—some hardly worthy of aid—who would otherwise go elsewhere. There is an increasing effort to link loans and scholarships so that not all the student aid is in the form of outright grants.

A small sampling of scholarship funds available in church-related colleges for the school year 1958–59 follows. These represent all types of accredited church-related senior colleges in four states.

SCHOLARSHIP FUNDS FOR 1958–59—SELECTED SENIOR COLLEGES

Institution	Enrollment	Scholarships Granted	Funds Used	Average Grant
1	839	252	$ 65,000	$258
2	2,182	533	$234,000	$437
3	1,004	169	$ 33,100	$196
4	1,616	266	$ 74,880	$281
5	582	80	$ 21,980	$275
6	412	94	$ 61,148	$650
7	535	25	$ 11,000	$440
8	1,823	193	$104,000	$540
9	1,745	464	$ 83,065	$177
10	431	65	$ 30,811	$473

The average scholarship among these colleges, from college funds, ranges from $177 to $650.

Campus Life

It is not possible in this brief treatment to attempt a characterization of student life on campuses of so wide a variety. Here are noted a few of the common features.

Residential colleges. In general the church-related college is a residential one in which a majority of students live on campus. Institutions in cities or part of urban areas are exceptions but there is a clear trend even in these to build more dormitory units. A large number of the junior colleges under study are mainly day schools, but even here the tendency is toward more campus housing.

Housing. The most dramatic physical change on many church-college campuses in the past decade has been the improvement in student housing. This has come about largely as a result of loans to colleges for the construction of dormitories. As a result, the living accommodations on these campuses are more attractive to students than ever before. The results of the program of federal loans for student centers, which may also include dining facilities, are only now being felt. One danger is inherent in the loan programs: Some colleges are finding that the new facilities are not completely self-supporting because of the increasing cost of construction.

Dormitories among these colleges tend to get larger and are therefore increasingly hard to manage. Very few are found, however, that do not house a matron entrusted with maintaining order and offering such counsel as she can. Most frequently these are not skilled or technically trained counselors but are older women who, it is hoped, will exert a "good influence" on the situation and who, in some cases, even dispense home remedies for their "boys and girls." In the more affluent institutions, however, there are trained counselors in each dormitory. In Catholic schools there are often members of the sponsoring community living on every floor of the dormitories.

The housing on the campuses of numerous Protestant senior colleges has become, by design or accident, partly the responsibility of social fraternities and sororities. In a relatively few institutions more students are cared for in fraternity and sorority houses than in college-owned buildings. A random sampling of a dozen colleges gives the following results. Only one of the sample group has sorority houses.

PERCENTAGE OF TOTAL STUDENT BODY IN COLLEGE-OWNED HOUSING AND IN FRATERNITY AND SORORITY HOUSES—RANDOM SAMPLING

Institution	Percent Dormitories	Percent Fraternity Houses
1	75	1
2	32	61
3	62	0
4	10	0
5	69	7
6	64	8
7	54	0
8	43	45
9	70	0
10	63	16
11	62	7
12	75	11

In these 12 Protestant institutions the number of students living in college housing ranges from 10 to 75 per cent and the number in fraternity and sorority houses from none to 61 per cent. In most fraternity houses today a matron is in residence and in about one-third of the cases the matron is on the college payroll.

Fraternity exclusiveness. The fraternity-sorority situation on

the campus of a church-related college represents more than a housing problem. The difficulty is related to the restrictive policies of
most national social organizations. Thus a college of repute which
states the following objective confronts at once in its fraternities
and sororities a violation of its own principles:

> As a Christian college, X University holds that discrimination on
> the basis of race, creed, or nationality is incompatible with its prin-
> ciples.

The problem is one which church-related colleges dare not continue
to neglect. It is no minor issue.

The fraternities and sororities bring with them both advantages
and disadvantages. The advantage is that they supply small, ready-
made social units which tend to overcome some of the difficulties of
large dormitories and large campuses. At their best they offer social
and cultural opportunities which can enrich the lives of individual
students. At their worst they may act as veto groups to hinder the
major objectives of the institution. They may so dominate a student
government as to render it unable to perform any important campus-
wide functions. When a campus has most of its students living in
fraternity and sorority housing, the problem is especially acute.

Religious life. The chapel services of the church-related college have long been a major point of debate. The Catholic college
position is clear: In Catholic institutions, Catholic students are expected to attend the Mass regularly, but Protestants are not required
to do so. Attendance at spiritual life retreats is also expected of
Catholics; others are invited but are not required to attend.

The Protestant college often takes a different stand. If chapel is
required, it is normally required for all. At times the sponsoring denomination is in a minority in the student body and a worship
service at which attendance is required will doubtless be serving
students of groups whose views may vary radically from those of the
sponsoring body. Catholic and Jewish students may find the services
highly distasteful, even though they know in advance of admission
that the college requires chapel attendance.

In a notable book published in 1947, Merrimon Cuninggim [3]
cogently expressed minimum essentials for effective chapel services,

---

[3] Merrimon Cuninggim, *The College Seeks Religion* (New Haven, Conn.: Yale
University Press, 1947), pp. 275 ff.

principles which are still important. His major points may be paraphrased as follows:

1. A college should provide opportunity for participation in *voluntary* worship services, whether or not chapel attendance is compulsory.

2. Chapel services should be disassociated from assembly programs.

3. Regardless of the form of service, it must be well planned. "Every time the chapel bell rings, religion as well as the college is on trial."

4. Every campus should have an adequate place for worship.

The trend toward the elimination of compulsory chapel continues, but it is a very slow movement. Among the 69 Methodist-related colleges included in this study, five institutions, for example, require chapel to every one which does not. The shift toward voluntaryism in this group has occurred in some cases because there is no chapel large enough to seat the entire student body. Numerous colleges, however, offer duplicate services. In some denominations there is almost no shift toward voluntary chapel.

Henry M. Wriston, former president of Lawrence College and Brown University, expresses in these words the general view of required chapel held by many church-related colleges:

> The second difficulty with college chapel has been a stupid confusion about what is "compulsory" and what is not. Though the curriculum has many requirements, they are never called "compulsory." Every student at Brown, whether he liked it or not, had to learn to swim before he could be graduated. There was plenty of dislike of the requirement among those who did not enjoy water, but no protest at "compulsory" swimming. The central fact is that students are not assigned to colleges; they choose them for reasons as various as could possibly be imagined. When they select a college which has published its requirements, they elect to do what it prescribes for the attainment of a degree—and, perchance, an education. That includes chapel if attendance is an announced feature of its life.[4]

There is no institution known to the author in which it is seriously held that worship itself can be "required." The hope is rather that inspiring music and liturgy may not only lead the student into an experience which will enrich his life, but may also prepare him at least to listen to thoughtful and, most commonly, nondenominational preaching.

---

[4] Henry M. Wriston, *Academic Procession* (New York: Columbia University Press, 1959), p. 197.

Most campuses now have one chapel service per week. Colleges have come gradually to understand that large captive audiences do not necessarily produce large results; or if they do, the results may be negative. It is also increasingly common to bring religious leaders to the campus for the entire community to hear.

Revival meetings have all but disappeared from the college scene except in a relatively few institutions sponsored by fundamentalist groups. "Religion in Life Weeks" still persist, however, though in a great variety of forms. Where once the program was almost exclusively preaching, it now tends to be made up as well of general treatments of religious questions—in panels, small group meetings, and regular class discussions.

Opportunities for students to take part in service projects are an important part of every effective campus religious program. These are usually sponsored by a Student Christian Association, which may be a federation of denominational student associations on the campus, or may itself be the single student religious organization. The projects may deal with local community problems, regional movements, or national and international efforts to attack serious social problems. Attendance by student leaders at regional and national conferences helps greatly to overcome the provincialism of the smaller, isolated campus.

The most effective campus religious organizations today exhibit some or all of the following characteristics:

1. Out-of-class study of the scriptures and the Christian heritage.
2. Deepened theological understanding of history and of the present.
3. Appreciation of the arts and growing interest in the expression of Christian insight through the arts.
4. Sharp sensitivity to major social, political, and international problems, especially in their entailment of responsibility for Christians.
5. A resurgent willingness to become "involved" and to take risks where they believe responsibility calls.
6. A developing resistance to the materialistic orientation of life and a growing interest in recovery of spiritual foundations.
7. Concern that the church recover its prophetic voice, break off its enfeebling identification with the existing order, and free itself from entrenched bureaucracy within.

In short, church-related colleges at their best are struggling to find new methods to carry out their special mission.

Discipline.   Student discipline in the church-related colleges

again shows a wide variety of forms. In many institutions discipline
is a function of a faculty committee on which nearly always sit the
personnel deans, the academic dean, and often the president. Many
discipline committees now include representative student members,
though student membership is likely to be in the minority. In general, expulsion for disciplinary reasons must be approved by the
president.

The regimentation which once characterized most small liberal
arts colleges still persists in some places, but in liberalized form.
Dormitory hours for girls remain relatively firm and, particularly in
the Catholic colleges for women, are rigid. Rules for class attendance are generally out-of-date in all types of institutions, and the
church college is no exception. Surely upper-class students at least
should be able to bear responsibility for their own class attendance.
In the more conservative communions, social dancing may still be
barred, though here too there are strange anomalies. Thus square
dancing may be permitted where social dancing is not.

One disciplinary problem, which appears to some peculiar to the
church college, is related to the use of alcohol. Here there is a considerable difference among institutions of various types. Catholic
institutions for men may disapprove of the use of alcoholic beverages in dormitories, but drunkenness is regarded as an enemy and is
seriously disciplined. For social functions the Catholic college for
men may take the following position, which represents a college in
the Northeast:

> It is the present policy of the college to tolerate the practice of
> conducting organizational meetings and affairs on campus premises
> at which beer is sold. Organizational officers are reminded, however,
> that club recognition depends crucially upon the manner in which
> such events are conducted. Any excess or carelessness will disqualify
> the organization for any future concessions of this type.
>
> Other campus or off-campus events conducted by student organi-
> zations at which alcoholic beverages stronger than beer are also
> served, will be approved but only rarely, for responsible groups, and
> with the most stringent safeguards for propriety and decorum. Un-
> der no circumstances are students permitted to *bring* such beverages
> to these affairs.

The above point of view may be compared with that of a Protestant college in the same region, and one which would be typical for
a large group:

The college may require withdrawal, without refunding fees, for any conduct which it considers undesirable, including the use or possession of alcoholic beverages on the campus or in any of its buildings or appearing under the influence of alcohol at any time.

Many of the liquor regulations grew from the official position of the founding church, and some institutions still maintain the rules because of their church affiliation. The current apprehension, however, grows more from the fear that, once the barriers are down officially, the problem of excess drinking in a closely-knit academic community will increase rapidly until it impairs the entire educational effort. For this reason a large number of institutions not related to churches, including public institutions, attempt to hold to no-drinking regulations.

The use of alcoholic beverages is but one illustration of the fact that the church-related college is often attempting to maintain a minority point of view regarding morals and social customs, even though the view may not be fully shared by their constituency. Studies indicate that drinking college students come mainly from drinking homes and from the homes of at least nominal church members. The obvious question follows: If the constituency no longer shares the views of the college on social problems, why should the college continue to struggle to maintain these attitudes? There are two answers to the question. One is that the "official" church may take a dim view of any shift in social standards, even though the rank and file of membership violates the official standards. The other reason has been noted in the previous paragraph. Educators seeing the spread of alcoholism and drunkenness, and fearing the effect upon educational efficiency of even temporizing with the problem, hold firm, or as firm as they can. There is no doubt that a college ought to make its regulations known before the student is admitted, but there is equally no doubt that it will grow increasingly difficult to maintain social standards which are out of line with popular norms.

Student government. The effort to involve the student body deeply in setting and controlling campus standards is worth all the difficulty it costs. There are church-related colleges in which the students are accepting increasing responsibility for the tone of the campus; there are others in which students have little or nothing to say about anything. In the latter instances, campuses serve as authoritarian, though often ineffective, forces upon most important educational possibilities.

Student government languishes at many places because no real authority or responsibility is given to it. On the other hand, students often dislike to take any more responsibility than absolutely necessary. They may not, for example, vote for an honor system because they do not wish to report their peers who cheat. There is a long fight ahead for students, faculty, and administrators to make the college years an adventure in mutual responsibility.

CHAPTER VII

The Financial Situation

Educational efforts are achieved primarily by strength of personnel—students, faculty, administration, and trustees. But financial vitality helps in a large measure to determine personnel. The financial problem of the church college grows increasingly acute even in the midst of what may appear to be more resources (and physical strength) than ever before. First, where does the money come from to operate church colleges? How is the money used?

In order to deal objectively with income and expense, the author uses here, as a large and more or less representative group, two- and four-year colleges related to the Methodist Church. These figures are available and relatively complete. The sampling includes 69 senior and 21 two-year colleges. The figures in each case are for the school year 1960–61.

Where the money comes from—senior colleges. Among the 69 four-year colleges in the group, median income from tuition and fees was 58.6 per cent of total educational and general income. The average was only slightly higher—58.8 per cent.

A percentage analysis of total income for educational and general purposes indicates the following:

PER CENT OF EDUCATIONAL AND GENERAL INCOME BY SOURCE
69 METHODIST SENIOR COLLEGES—1960–61

Source	Average Per Cent
Tuition and fees	58.8
Edowment earnings	10.0
Gifts and grants	23.7
Other	2.7
Net on auxiliary	4.8

The median and average income percentages are useful, but the extreme represented by individual cases will illustrate again the wide diversities among church-related colleges.

| | Percentages | |
Source	High	Low
Tuition and fees	89.5	23.7
Endowment earnings	35.9	1.8
Gifts and grants	76.4	7.1
Net on auxiliary	27.9	Minus[1]

Thus there are Methodist-related colleges which receive more than 80 per cent of their total current income from tuition and fees. Eight of the 69 colleges receive 75 per cent or more of current income from this source. Each of these is in an urban setting and each enrolls more than 1,000 students. Eighteen colleges, on the other hand, report less than 50 per cent of current income from student fees. Most of these are below 600 in enrollment and are in small towns rather than in large cities.

Endowment income is still important and every college in the group is trying to increase its endowment holdings. Six of the institutions receive more than 25 per cent of current educational and general income from endowments, while sixteen receive less than 5 per cent from this source.

There are large variations in current income from gifts and grants. The high of 76.4 per cent from this source is reported by a new college in its second year of operation. Twenty-seven, or more than one-third of the senior colleges, report over 20 per cent of total income from gifts and grants, while eleven report less than 5 per cent from this source. That more than one fourth of the colleges report losses on auxiliary enterprises raises serious questions regarding institutional philosophy of management.

It may be useful to compare a few of these categories with *The Sixty College Study* which was prepared for the years 1953–54 and updated in *The Sixty College Study—A Second Look* for the school year 1957–58.[2] The revision dealt with but 56 of the original 60 private colleges of various types in all parts of the country. Brief comparisons in selected items with the Methodist sample follow:

---

[1] Eighteen of the institutions, or over one-fourth, reported losses on auxiliary enterprises in 1960–61.

[2] National Federation of College and University Business Officers, *The Sixty College Study—A Second Look* (New York: Columbia University Press 1960).

AVERAGES FOR METHODIST COLLEGE SAMPLE AND 56 COLLEGES
PER CENT OF EDUCATIONAL AND GENERAL INCOME

	Methodist Sample	56 Colleges
Tuition and fees	58.8	56.8
Endowment earnings	10.0	20.7
Gifts and grants	23.7	17.6

Thus the Methodist sample on the average is more heavily dependent than the 56-college group upon tuition and fees along with gifts and grants, but Methodist schools receive less from endowment income. The large proportion of institutions in the sample of 56 is made up of relatively high endowment institutions.

How the money is spent. For the same 69 Methodist senior colleges, expenditure by percentage for educational and general purposes is as follows:

PER CENT OF EDUCATIONAL AND GENERAL EXPENDITURES
69 METHODIST SENIOR COLLEGES

Function	Median	Average
Administration and general	26.9	27.8
Instruction	50.0	49.2
Library	4.4	4.7
Plant operation and maintenance	15.3	15.7
Miscellaneous	1.4	2.6

Again there are wide differences among institutions as the following chart of *high* and *low* percentages indicates:

EXPENDITURE BY FUNCTION—HIGH AND LOW

	Percentage [3]	
Function	High	Low
Administration and general	37.6	13.0
Instruction	61.3	31.3
Library	7.6	2.3
Plant operation and maintenance	25.1	6.0

The smaller institutions show the highest administrative costs, and the colleges with new or rebuilt plants show the lowest operation and maintenance costs.

Two-year college figures. Two-year colleges related to the Methodist Church produce the following figures:

---

[3] These figures do not include three new four-year colleges, one in Alaska.

PER CENT OF EDUCATIONAL AND GENERAL INCOME BY SOURCE
21 METHODIST TWO-YEAR COLLEGES, 1960–61

Averages

Tuition and fees	53.1
Endowment earnings	4.7
Gifts and grants	28.4
Other	1.7
Net on auxiliaries	12.1

PER CENT OF EDUCATIONAL AND GENERAL EXPENDITURES
21 METHODIST TWO-YEAR COLLEGES, 1960–61

Averages

Administration and general	29.5
Instruction	41.0
Library	4.6
Plant operation and maintenance	22.2
Miscellaneous	2.7

Endowments

Endowments were for many years the mainstay of the private institution, and even today they represent an important resource. As costs have risen, however, endowment income has been a proportionately less significant factor among both church-related colleges and other private institutions. Many of the Methodist group were not originally well-endowed.

To use the Methodist sector as a sample again, the following figures indicate the present endowment structure of the four-year institutions referred to earlier (see p. 19). The largest endowment in the group in 1961 was $13,000,000 (book value) while the smallest was slightly in excess of $400,000. Not included among these are institutions attended primarily by Negroes, and in some instances still "owned" by church agencies.

Highly significant is the endowment per student, which gives a more accurate indication than the gross amount of endowment capital gives of what help may actually be expected from endowment sources. The following chart shows the position of the 69 Methodist colleges for the academic year 1960–61:

Highest	$13,307
Median	$ 2,137
Lowest	$ 275

The median institution could anticipate only about $85 per student from endowment income, while the college with the highest endowment could expect about $532 per student. The figures used here deal only with book values which were in almost every instance markedly lower than market value on January 1, 1963.

Church contributions. Closely related to endowment income is that from gifts and grants for current operations. This is a type of living endowment. Where endowment income for this group of colleges averaged 10 per cent of educational and general income, gifts and grants averaged 23.7 per cent.

In the relation of gifts and grants to educational and general income, however, there is a wide disparity among institutions. The lowest is 7.1 per cent of educational and general income; the highest is 76.4 per cent. Of major interest here are the direct contributions of church bodies to the institutions they sponsor. Illustrations of systematic current church support are given in the following profiles taken from various church groups:

Institution A is a Midwest, Methodist college enrolling slightly over 2,000 students in 1961. Its educational and general income is approximately $2,000,000 and it receives gifts and grants in excess of $300,000. Of this amount $100,000 is directly from church sources. This compares with less than $2,000 from the same source in 1940. The $100,000 would pay the salaries of ten faculty members at $10,000 each, which is somewhat above the present college average. There are Methodist colleges which receive more and many which receive less. Since the college is planning a capital funds campaign, direct church sources will doubtless produce at least $1,000,000.

Institution B is a Protestant Episcopal college for men in the South, enrolling in 1961 some 600 students. Its educational and general income for the same year was just over $1,000,000, of which not quite 50 per cent came from student fees. The direct income from the church for current expenses was $183,000 as compared with $20,000 in 1940. The 1960–61 church grant represents in excess of 18 per cent of the educational and general income. For capital expenditures in the same year the church contributed $137,000.

Institution C is a Catholic college for men in the Southwest, enrolling in 1961 approximately 500 students. Most Catholic colleges receive no contributions directly from church sources. Exceptions are the diocesan colleges which are a small minority of the total. Institution *C* received no direct funds from the church but sought support from leading Catholic laymen as well as from non-Catholics.

Institution D is a Presbyterian college in the Midwest, enrolling some 800 students in 1961. Its current support from its denomination was about $50,000 for an educational and general budget of $650,000. This represents about 8 per cent of the total. It is, however, an increase from $5,000 in 1945.

Institution E is an American Baptist college on the West coast, enrolling 1,700 students in 1961. Of an educational and general income of $2,600,000, about $30,000 (or slightly over 1 per cent) came directly from church sources. The president notes, however, that other contributions came from Baptists individually.

Institution F is a Lutheran college in the Midwest, enrolling in 1961 over 1,300 students. The educational and general income was just over $1,000,000, with church sources contributing $184,000 or about 18 per cent. The college in the same year received $431,000 from church sources for capital improvements.

Institution G is a Southern Baptist college in the Southeast, enrolling 1,300 students in 1961. Of a general and educational income of $1,500,000, nearly $200,000 (or about 13 per cent) came directly from church sources.

These illustrations could be multiplied many times, but with the same tendencies in evidence. Direct church support for current operations varies from almost nothing to as much as 20 per cent of educational and general income. Church bodies appear, however, to be growing more keenly aware of their opportunities and responsibilities in higher education. The danger that some of the new enthusiasm may be spent in founding new institutions before the old are properly undergirded has already been noted.

There are few useful guides as to what church support ought to be. Only as an effort to suggest a direction for thought about the problem, the author proposes that churches consider the following guidelines. In 1954 a study group noted that the cost of educating a student in 1952–53, beyond what the student paid, was in the Protestant church-related colleges about $344 and in the Catholic colleges about $239.[4] Since that time the difference between cost and student charges is even greater. The author suggests that an accredited senior college ought to have available from all sources other than tuition at least $400 per student, and that a junior college ought to have at least half this amount. If the college is unaccredited, much more is required to bring it up to a bare minimum. The related church ought to resolve to meet the suggested sum of $400 per student, through income from endowments, gifts, grants, and other sources. A college poorly endowed would need more gifts and grants than one substantially endowed. If a church college generates no capability of attracting other sources of funds, the church may perhaps conclude that the college is too weak to develop as it should.

There is no magic in the suggested $400 and it cannot remain fixed, but it might be used as a starting point for some kind of intelligent calculation of institutional need. All sources of income must be exploited to the full, and no single body can be alone responsible for outside support. It is only in a broad base of support, including church support, that private institutional freedom will be protected.

Plant and Equipment

Plants of church-related colleges have changed astonishingly for the better over the past decade. This generalization cannot be applied universally, yet it is true for perhaps 80 per cent of all church-college campuses. Listed below are the reported book values of a group of senior church-related colleges selected at random. The list includes colleges related to numerous churches and both accredited and unaccredited institutions.

---

[4] Council for the Financial Aid to Education, Inc., *What Price Tuition*, November, 1957, p. 2.

BOOK VALUES OF PHYSICAL PLANTS—1940, 1950, 1960

Institution	1940	1950	1960
1. Southeast	$ 947,000	$1,744,000	$5,789,000
2. Midwest	1,162,000	2,856,000	5,270,000
3. Northcentral	216,000	351,000	603,000
4. South	939,000	2,010,000	8,200,000
5. Far West	1,882,000	2,056,000	5,805,000
6. Northwest	905,000	2,057,000	5,100,000
7. Midwest	1,800,000	3,100,000	8,579,000
8. Southwest	——	500,000	2,730,000
9. Northeast	2,065,000	3,842,000	8,151,000
10. Southeast	1,568,000	2,950,000	5,896,000
11. Northcentral	290,000	569,000	1,425,000
12. Great Plains	330,000	892,000	1,655,000

The federal loan programs for dormitories and student unions have helped in the advances noted in the table. But close scrutiny of developments indicates that—while dormitories and unions represent a major part of recent construction—libraries, fine arts centers, chapels, classroom buildings, and science halls are very heavily represented.

That indebtedness has gone along with the advances is also clear. An examination of the church-related colleges of five states indicates that indebtedness ranges from 10 per cent of plant valuation to as high as 33 per cent. Institutions with the higher ranges are mainly urban colleges which have gone very heavily into such self-amortizing buildings as dormitories and student unions. Unfortunately it has not been possible to separate self-liquidating projects in these indebtedness figures.

Library Expenditures

The data are not available to analyze in detail the expenditure patterns of a majority of church-related colleges, but a glance at one area—the libraries of these institutions—can give some indication of shifting educational standards. Seventy senior colleges were selected at random to indicate the current collections to be found on the campuses under study.

Of the 70 colleges, there were 10 which had collections of 100,000 volumes or over, the largest being 198,000. Another 6 had collections which numbered 80,000 or more, and 15 others boasted collections of over 50,000 volumes. The median collection among the sample of 70 was 45,500 volumes. The smallest library was 12,000 volumes in a senior college just changing from junior college status and still regionally unaccredited.

The last decade has seen a strong growth in the libraries of the group, both in volumes purchased and in expenditures for new books. It is not uncommon to find institutions today spending three times as much for new books as they did a decade ago. Yet there are still far too many senior colleges, even with regional accreditation, which are not able to build collections as they should.

Tuition and Fees

As pointed out in previous chapters, the financial problem of the church-related college is generally serious and is likely to grow more so unless new sources of funds are discovered. Tuition and fees have been rising steadily and, in some instances, with great rapidity—an indication that competitively the church-related college is not even holding its own financially. The key to this generalization is to be found in the faculty salary problem (see Chapter V).

As students pay more and more of the costs of their own education and as the percentages of income from student fees have shown, they will properly expect more and more from the colleges. Yet when a college is forced to pay its faculty $1,000 to $2,000 less than competing institutions, it is difficult to get the people who can produce the best results. This is the basis of the problem, and it represents the major challenge of the future to church-related colleges. There is much that can be done to become more efficient and less wasteful; but efficiency alone will never solve the fundamental problems of increasing tuitions and potentially decreasing quality. New resourcefulness is a requirement of the future.

CHAPTER VIII

Prospect and Revision

Generalizations in Summary

The following factors appear to be critical in the church-related college situation today:

1. About one-third of all degree-granting and two-year colleges in the United States have some sort of relationship to a church body. These relationships vary greatly.

2. The variety among church-related institutions is exceptionally great, both in philosophy and in quality. The median enrollment of the four-year colleges in this study is 663; of the two-year institutions it is 185. It is doubtful that the median represents the most economical operating unit for senior colleges.

3. About 9 per cent of church-related four-year colleges lack regional accreditation, but only five of these have an enrollment of more than 600. The accreditation picture regarding the junior colleges is much poorer, approximating 40 per cent of the total. A college long unaccredited must be considered a reproach to its sponsor.

4. There is considerable divergence among the colleges as to their basic purposes and functions. If there is a common cause among them, it is this: a dedication to the cultivation of mind and spirit. By cultivation of the mind is meant the development of those intellectual powers and virtues which are accepted by all colleges and universities as their first responsibility. There is a popular fear that many church-related institutions do not give themselves fully to this difficult and complex task. The fear would seem justified in too many instances.

By cultivation of the spirit is meant the development of the self-critical, self-judging powers. The goal, however stated, requires that the student again and again be vitally confronted with the fundamental questions of human life. It is at this point that the church-related college seeks to differ from those which regard the intellectual virtues as the sole end of education.

This end is immensely difficult to achieve, since it involves not merely official purpose but faculty members and students as well. These come to the campus with their own assumptions and educational ideals. Thus faculty and student selection and orientation are always a critical problem for a college.

5. The cultivation of mind and spirit in a Christian context requires that the student be brought into contact with the tradition out of which this context has developed. The characteristic church-related college attempts to confront the student wherever possible with the demands of the Judaeo-Christian tradition. This task is approached in a variety of ways, from rigorous study of the Bible and required attendance at the Mass or at chapel, to Christian service opportunities of many types.

In the effort to infuse campus life with the demands of the Judaeo-Christian tradition, the colleges show their widest variety. Colleges related to fundamentalist groups will approach the problem in one way; those related to liberal groups, in quite another. The Catholic approach will be different from the Protestant.

The author holds that it is fully within the right of the college to determine its own method of meeting this objective, so long as it does not thereby render ineffective its grave responsibility for intellectual goals. If a choice has to be made between a college which is clear in its intellectual demands but less concerned about "cultivation of the spirit," and another institution which neglects its intellectual role, surely the former is the honest one. A college without intellectual sincerity is no college at all.

6. While most church-related colleges consider the liberal arts as their fundamental responsibility, there are too many which have catered for opportunistic reasons to certain types of vocationalism and have allowed their programs to become pale imitations of the larger secular university.[1] The result has been a bloated curriculum, an inefficiency in use of resources and personnel, and a confused educational goal. There appears to be a movement toward return to the liberal arts.

7. Since the power of an educational institution is finally and

---

[1] The author assumes no dogmatic position regarding vocationalism. For most students, life implies life in a job, and students are concerned about their careers. Colleges of sharply limited resources cannot do everything. They must therefore decide what they can do best within the context of their liberal arts commitments.

irrevocably determined by its personnel—especially teachers and students—the church-related college will find its chief difficulty in the years ahead in the recruitment of strong faculties. This is a direct reflection of the financial weakness of many colleges in the group. Outstanding teachers attract exciting students.

Salaries in church-related colleges tend to fall well below those of competing institutions, often even in the median colleges to as much as $2,500 below public institutions. While today the training of numerous church-college faculties may still compare favorably with what is found in other types of institutions, the ultimate result of a salary differential is altogether obvious. Experience over the years has shown that there are sizable numbers of teachers who want to teach in a religiously oriented institution, yet in a day of inflation salaries are crucial. It is at this point that the future of the church college is most in jeopardy. An obvious corollary is that the best students will increasingly select those colleges with the best faculties.

8. Physically the "average" church-related college is better off than at any time in its history. Many who comment on the educational scene have not recently examined the colleges they are talking about, and their observations are relevant only to yesterday. While there are still many church colleges badly equipped and physically ill-fitted to their tasks, there are large numbers which are growing stronger and stronger physically. Federal loan programs have helped greatly, but they are not solely responsible for recent improvements.

9. Far too many church-related colleges are now heavily dependent on student fees, and to the degree that this is true the college is handicapped in establishing and realizing any unique goals.

Thus colleges which were founded to provide education for the poor may in the near future, if not already, find themselves able to educate only the privileged. This is a clear danger at the present time.

Imperatives

What must the church-related college do to retain its opportunity for distinctive service in the future? What must the sponsors of church-related colleges do if their institutions are to continue to make a useful contribution to American life? The author proposes the following "imperatives" which in one way or another involve both institutions and sponsors.

1. Every church-related college must re-appraise its true academic quality. There can be no compromise with this demand for intellectual rigor. Obviously not everything can be done with limited funds, but what is attempted ought to be done well. This is therefore a demand for restraint within the academic community itself.

There is a long history of excellence among church-related colleges which will stand close scrutiny. A few exhibits can make the point clear.

> A. In the Knapp-Greenbaum study of proportionate production of male Ph.D.'s, church colleges in the group under study represented 16 of the top 50.[2]
> B. In the Knapp-Goodrich study of proportionate production of American scientists, 12 of the first 25 institutions were church colleges represented in this study, as were 16 of the second 25. Thus 28 of the top 50 colleges were church-related.[3]
> C. In the Pfnister studies on baccalaureate origins of college faculties, 19 of the top 50 producers were church-related colleges.[4]
> D. For the triennium 1961–64 there were 190 institutions having Phi Beta Kappa chapters in the United States. If the universities are taken from the list, 93 colleges remain, of which 37 are church-related and are represented in this study.

Other studies might be cited with approximately the same results evident for church colleges. These are institutions in which the intellectual has been emphasized. These records, however, stand in serious jeopardy in the future unless the colleges more strongly assert their intellectual goals.

2. Colleges should not all be alike, nor should they slavishly imitate one another. A church-related college should therefore aim to be its best self, meeting as well as it can the needs of its region and of its constituency.

There is a popular tendency today to assume that as colleges grow

---

[2] Robert H. Knapp and Joseph J. Greenbaum, *The Younger American Scholar: His Collegiate Origins* (Chicago: University of Chicago Press, 1953), pp. 16–17.

[3] Robert H. Knapp and H. B. Goodrich, *Origins of American Scientists* (Chicago: University of Chicago Press, 1952), p. 22.

[4] Allan O. Pfnister, *A Report of the Baccalaureate Origins of College Faculties* (Washington, D.C.: Association of American Colleges, 1961), pp. 30–31.

more and more selective, they automatically produce increasingly
significant results. The fundamental test ought to be: How far does
the college take the students it has? What changes does it produce
in students? Are the changes desirable? Thus one institution may
take only high scorers on College Entrance Examination Board tests
and change students very little. Another institution may take far less
mentally sophisticated or able students and help move them farther
along toward becoming more enlightened, more fully responsible
individuals. It will be a sad day if all private colleges decide that
prestige is what they seek. The imperative here is that the college
determine its mission, do its best to meet it, and study very carefully
the results of its work.

3. The church-related college should rededicate itself to the task
it is most capable of performing—the development of liberal arts
education. While this term is not self-explanatory, its underlying
ideals are more widely understood than honored. Church-related
colleges as a group may indeed become one of the few last substantial defenders of liberal education. This means that every type of
vocationalism must be carefully examined with a view to ascertain-
ing what relationship, if any, it has to liberal arts education. In line
with this imperative is an equal need for a church college not to
claim more than it can produce, and not to spread itself so thin that
its energies and resources are dissipated in superficialities.

4. The church college must remember that when it attempts to
cultivate the "spirit," however construed, it is attemping what many
institutions regard as impossible. This is the point of uniqueness of
church-related colleges, and while the task must be approached with
humility, it is none the less significant to the whole educational enterprise. It is imperative therefore that the college resolve not to settle
for intellectual goals alone—though never underestimating their
validity—but to understand the tremendous responsibility it has
accepted. New approaches to this problem are essential. Especially
must the college and the sponsoring church understand one another
and labor together to produce a plan and a program of sufficient
stature to serve as a symbol to all American higher education.

5. The church-related colleges in this sample are small institutions by current standards, though the variation in size among them
may be substantial. As smaller institutions they have certain advantages. They can develop a sense of community if they fully exploit

their size. They can change more readily than the large institution in which power structures are complex and difficult to deal with. They are far more susceptible to vigorous leadership than the large complexes. They can make fruitful dialogue possible among all sectors of the academic community. They can develop a campus tone which exhibits moral concern along with intellectual excellence.

The smaller institution, however, faces equally great hazards. The college may become so regimented and so regulated that personal growth is seriously hampered. The college may allow no room for rebellious youngsters, who disappear more readily into the broad stream of a large community. If the college is too small, it may find itself with a collection of one-man departments. This may lead to serious faculty overloads and lack of stimulation. Today, one man can not profitably cover the whole area encompassed by a major discipline, nor is the give-and-take between student and discipline likely to occur where only one man speaks for the field. It is imperative, therefore, that the smallest colleges be brought to a more effective size and that every possible method be employed to withstand the dangers of provincialism.

6. It must be apparent that church relationship does not necessarily mean adequate church support. It may, in fact, mean little more than token support. Every church-related college must find substantial funds from sources other than the church if it succeeds. It is imperative, therefore, that churches which support colleges on any level reconsider their responsibilities:

> A. If a college has long remained unaccredited, the church ought to face the possibility that the college is inherently too weak to survive at an honest level of quality. If such an institution is continued, the church must resolve to make significant and perhaps painful efforts to bring the college up to minimum standards. Can any church dare sponsor poor education which in the long run handicaps the students it purports to serve?
> B. Churches of similar philosophy must find new ways of cooperation in higher education. This is already being done in some places.
> C. The churches must re-examine their role in defending academic freedom in a day of shifting economic and social conditions. This is a privilege and an obligation, not a burden.
> D. Churches which sponsor education institutions must support more heavily the superior institution (with all the problems academic strength entails) and not neglect these in order to help the

weak, more subservient college. This requires maturity, of both college and church, and a clear view of the issues.

Prospects

The administrators of most of the institutions with which this study has dealt are sharply aware of the decisive nature of the times, so far as church colleges are concerned. The large majority are committed to the special mission of the church college. They appreciate the difficulty of their task. They are also conscious of the easy tendency to substitute a spurious piety for sound academic work; yet they believe almost to an individual that cultivation of mind and spirit in some religious sense is possible and necessary for the nation.

These leaders are committed to their churches, and they are eager to serve faithfully. They are, however, often at a loss to find the means to make church leaders understand the true nature of the present crisis. Presidents understand the rising cost of higher education, but their constituencies do not. Moreover, presidents doubt that church leaders comprehend fully either the possibility or the difficulty of the task to which the church-related college is committed. Educators in secular institutions also often misunderstand and ignore the educational issues posed by church-related colleges.

There is almost universal agreement that present survival is not the first issue. The problem is basically one of *quality* of survival. The point has been well-made by one president of a church-related college in the Midwest: "The challenge will be to keep before the college community an educational program which will engage faculty and students in an academic enterprise of very real quality. There is no distinction in being a small church-related college. The distinction comes in being *good* in all areas of the educational program."

Church-college leaders know that there will be enough students in the immediate future to require the best service of every sound institution. The problem is less whether there will be students than whether the church college can be strong enough to attract the promising student in sufficient numbers. There is full awareness that to a large degree students make the college. The presidents, in short, foresee the danger of a dual system of education divided between strong and weak, rather than between public and private. Some institutions sense already that their best students are impatient with the small demands made upon them by teachers whose standards are less than they should be.

The fundamental educational views of those engaged in the administration of church-related colleges are these: The future of the church-related college depends upon its ability to keep a clear view of its mission; upon its ability to find the church support needed to supplement other sources of income; and upon its success in interpreting its goals to students, faculty, constituency, and the general public.

Revision and Renewal

A fundamental test of an educational institution is its ability to renew its commitments and, at the same time, to blaze new educational trails. One of the most encouraging signs among a growing sector of church-related colleges is the willingness to return to fundamentals as the institutions start upon new paths. The following illustrations of educational developments among some church-related colleges in the nineteen sixties are selective but not exceptional; they represent all types of church colleges.

1. Three church colleges in one region now share a specialist who conducts work in Asian studies each term on each campus, and carries on a seminar for faculty members from the three institutions.

2. A college in the far West has cut its course offerings by 30 per cent, has developed four-year cycles of independent studies in seven areas, and has eliminated nearly all vocational programs and degrees.

3. A college in the Midwest has established a plan of freshman seminars in English required of all students, fifteen students in each seminar. The emphasis is upon developing the student's ability to help himself and to begin early to engage in independent study. In addition, the college is developing a four-year sequence of honors work stemming from the freshman English seminars.

4. A college for women in the East closes its on-campus sessions for five weeks beginning in November, during which time all students carry on some special activity—freshmen working in some community agency, sophomores doing cultural research or study, juniors and seniors working in fields related to their majors. There is also a program enrolling twenty to twenty-five students to work in Europe, Latin America, and India, with scholarship aid to meet all or part of transportation costs.

5. A college in the Midwest has embarked on a year-round course of study, with staggered quarters off campus for the student to engage in study or field work. Quarters are eleven weeks, with each student carrying a maximum of three courses on campus at one time. A $2,000,000 endowment will make possible foreign study for all students without extra cost.

6. A college in the Great Plains region has brought to its campus a colony of forty African students with their families. Each family is supported and sponsored by a local church. The plan has had an electric influence upon the whole region.

7. A college in the far West has built two of a series of cluster colleges to exploit more fully the intellectual opportunities of the academic community. One is a Latin American school with nearly all classes conducted in Spanish. These are colleges within a college, somewhat comparable to the "house" systems of a few eastern schools.

8. A new institution in the Southeast has developed an interdepartmental program involving team teaching of a core course entitled "Christianity and Culture." The course extends through four years and comprehensively integrates history, philosophy, and religion.

9. A small-town college in the Midwest has arranged an exchange program with Christ Church College of Oxford University. The American institution will send a senior graduate to Oxford each year; the English college will send a faculty member to teach in the Midwestern school.

Obviously a church-related college involves also what has been called a "college-related church." It has never been easy, on any level, to rationalize educational goals for the laymen. Too many churchmen are not fully aware of the true possibilities of higher education. They often support colleges for reasons which have little to do with educational excellence and which are at times actual barriers to quality.

There are signs in the nineteen sixties, however, that the churches through their educational boards and local leadership are beginning to ask the right questions again. As communication and understanding grow, there is hope that church and college can in fact work fruitfully together. If such an understanding can be achieved, the churches will find that through their colleges they can ask the entire university community the crucial questions regarding the ends of education.

Bibliography

Brown, Kenneth I., *Not Minds Alone*. New York: Harper & Row, Publishers, 1954.

Carpenter, Marjorie, ed., *The Larger Learning*. Dubuque, Iowa: William C. Brown Company, 1960.

Cuninggim, Merrimon, *The College Seeks Religion*. New Haven, Conn.: Yale University Press, 1947.

Ellis, John Tracy, *American Catholics and the Intellectual Life*. Chicago: Heritage Foundation, 1956.

Ensley, F. Gerald, *The Marks of Christian Education*. New York and Nashville, Tenn.: The Methodist Publishing House, 1958.

Ferre, Nels F., *Christian Faith and Higher Education*. New York: Harper & Row, Publishers, 1934.

Fuller, Edmund, ed., *The Christian Idea of Education*. New Haven, Conn.: Yale University Press, 1957.

Gross, John O., *Education for Life*. New York and Nashville, Tenn.: Abingdon Press, 1947.

Livingstone, Sir Richard, *On Education*. New York: The Macmillan Company, 1945.

Lowry, Howard, *The Mind's Adventure*. Philadelphia: Westminster Press, 1950.

Martorana, S. V., *College Boards of Trustees*. Washington, D.C.: The Center for Applied Research in Education, Inc., 1963.

Mayhew, Lewis B., *The Smaller Liberal Arts College*. Washington, D.C.: The Center for Applied Research in Education, Inc., 1962.

McCluskey, Neil (S.J.), *Catholic Viewpoint on Education*. Garden City, N. Y.: Hanover House, 1959.

Miller, Alexander, *Faith and Learning*. New York: Association Press, 1960.

Nef, John, *A Search for Civilization*. Chicago: Henry Regnery Co., 1962.

O'Dea, Thomas F., *American Catholic Dilemma: An Inquiry Into the Intellectual Life*. New York: Sheed & Ward, 1958.

Patton, Leslie K., *The Purposes of Church-Related Colleges*. New York: Teachers College, Columbia University, 1940.

Snavely, Guy E., *The Church and the Four-Year College: An Appraisal of Their Relation*. New York: Harper & Row, Publishers, 1955.

APPENDIX

Name of Institution_____

QUESTIONNAIRE

1. Describe in a few sentences the major purposes of your institution. Attach any more lengthy statement of purpose which may be available in print.
2. Who participated in formulating these purposes? When were they prepared?
3. Are these purposes in any way distinctive because the institution is church-related? Please be as specific as possible.
4. The board of trustees numbers_____.
   Of the total board how many are
   > *elected* by some denominational body?_____
   > *approved* by some denominational body?_____
   > *nominated* by some denominational body?_____
5. Please list additions to the physical plant within the last ten years, and indicate the cost of each addition and the source of the funds.
6. If the institution has plans for the construction of any new buildings in the next five years, please discuss these plans briefly, including the expenditure proposed for each building.
7. Has the institution made systematic studies of any phases of its program during the past five years?_____ If so, please list such studies and attach a copy of as many of the reports as are available.
8. Please give the number of persons in each of the following ranks (full-time only):

   _____Professors   _____Instructors

   _____Associate Professors   _____Assistants

   _____Assistant Professors   _____Other ranks of
                                            teaching personnel

9. Is there a written constitution or handbook for the faculty? If so, please attach a copy to this form.
10. How many faculty meetings were held during the last academic year?_____

107

11. What are the policies for the granting of tenure to members of the faculty?

12. What special limitations, if any, does the institution place on freedom of teaching? Are there, for example, limitations on the political, economic, or religious doctrines that may be taught in the institution? Please explain the reasons for any limitations adopted.

13. What proportion of the faculty represent the denomination supporting the institution?_____per cent.

14. Please describe briefly the role usually played by each of the following in the selection and appointment of new faculty members:
    A. Board of trustees
    B. President
    C. The dean
    D. The head of the department or division concerned.

15. Does the institution have a definite plan for granting leaves of absence to members of the teaching staff?_____If so, please give the following information about the plan: Who is eligible for leave; length and frequency of leaves; remuneration during leave; number of persons actually on leave during last two years; and the *number of persons actually on leave during these two years.*

16. If the institution has a retirement plan, please describe the provisions of the plan.

17. If the institution provides faculty housing or assists faculty members to secure housing, please describe these services.

18. Please give average salaries for the various ranks for the years listed:

	1940–41	1950–51	1955–56	1960–61
Professor				
Associate Professor				
Assistant Professor				
Instructor				

19. Enrollment:
    1. Please give the enrollments of the institution for each of the following years, omitting the summer session.

College Level Students Only

	1940–41	1950–51	1955–56	1960–61
Full-time students				
Freshmen				
Sophomores				
Juniors				
Seniors				

A. Total full-time
B. Part-time students
C. Part-time students
   equated to
   full-time
D. Total enrollment
   (A plus C)

2. Give the number of your students who are living on campus this term._____

20. Please list the states and foreign countries from which your student body for the present academic year is drawn and give the number of students from each state and country.

21. What are the requirements which all students regardless of field of specialization must meet in order to secure a bachelor's degree from your institution?

22. Please comment on any curricular features or devices that you feel distinguish your institution from others. Have there been any recent innovations or significant changes in curriculum that should be noted? Has the institution been particularly successful in its use of any special methods, such as comprehensive examinations, tutorials, independent study plan, integrative courses, or senior seminars or papers? Any published materials on these important matters will be helpful.

23. Does the institution have exact information about the aptitude of its students in comparison with the aptitude of students in other colleges and universities? For example, do you know the median aptitude of your students on the basis of one of the widely used tests such as the ACE, CEEB, ACT? If you have such information, please summarize it here. To what use is this information put? If the college publishes a profile of the freshman class, please include a copy.

24. Has the institution made any systematic studies of the success of its graduates in vocational, professional, religious, civic, or other respects after the completion of their formal education? If such studies have been made, please summarize the findings.

25. The Library:
    A. Number of volumes, exclusive of public documents.

       1940–41
       1950–51
       1955–56
       1960–61

B. How many books were accessioned last year?

C. How many periodicals are regularly taken?

D. How many newspapers are currently received?

E. Please list any significant changes in your library building in the last ten years.

F. Please give library expenditures for the following purposes for the years indicated:

	1940–41	1950–51	1955–56	1960–61
Books, pamphlets, and periodicals				
Binding and rebinding				
Salaries of library personnel (including part-time workers and student assistants)				
Supplies and equipment (excluding operation and care of building)				

Note: If it is not possible to secure all of the above figures from your records, please begin where you can.

G. How many full-time *professionally* trained librarians does the institution have?

H. Has the library staff made any comparative study of the use of the library by the students?_____If so, please summarize the results.

I. Please discuss briefly any features of the library which you feel merit special mention.

26. Does the institution place any limitation on the size of its student body or on the number of students that will be admitted to the freshman class or to any division or curriculum? Please discuss briefly any limiting policies that have been adopted.

27. Which of the following classes of students are given preference in the awarding of scholarships, the remission of fees, or the granting of other types of financial aid?   Others (please specify):

Children of staff members

Children of ministers

Athletes

High-ranking students, regardless of need

Needy students, regardless of academic record

High-ranking, needy students

28. What percentage of your students live in buildings operated by the institution?_____In fraternity and sorority houses?_____In off-campus rooming and boarding houses?_____At home?_____
29. How large is the campus in acres?_____
30. Please give book value of plant for the following years:

    1940–41
    1945–46
    1950–51
    1955–56
    1960–61

31. Please list the major plant needs of the immediate future along with costs involved. (See question 7)
32. Please give tuition and major fees and room and board costs, for the average A.B. student for each of the following years:

	Tuition and Fees	Room and Board
1940–41		
1945–46		
1950–51		
1955–56		
1960–61		

33. Please list below current and capital gifts from your denomination for the following years:

	Current	Capital
1940–41		
1945–46		
1950–51		
1955–56		
1960–61		

34. What are the major opportunities of your college in the decade ahead? What are the hazards of the future?

                    Signature and title of person responsible for returning questionnaire:

Signature	Title

Index

116